ANFIELD SOUTH

ANFIELD SOUTH

75 YEARS OF LIVERPOOL AT WEMBLEY

BRIAN BARWICK OBE

pitch

First published by Pitch Publishing, 2025
1

Pitch Publishing
9 Donnington Park,
85 Birdham Road,
Chichester, West Sussex,
PO20 7AJ

www.pitchpublishing.co.uk
info@pitchpublishing.co.uk

A CIP catalogue record is available for this book from the British Library.

ISBN 978 1 83680 155 9

Typesetting and origination by Pitch Publishing

FSC www.fsc.org MIX Paper | Supporting responsible forestry FSC™ C016779

Printed and bound on FSC® certified paper in line with our continuing commitment to ethical business practices, sustainability and the environment.

Printed and bound in India by Replika Press Pvt. Ltd.

Contents

To Bill Shankly's Boys of '65 –
Lawrence, Lawler, Byrne, Strong,
Yeats, Stevenson, Callaghan, Hunt, St
John, Smith, Thompson and Milne –
Wembley winners – heroes all!

Acknowledgements

FROM SHANKLY to Slot, King Kenny to Klopp, Liverpool Football Club's regular excursions to Wembley Stadium down through the decades have provided Reds' fans the world over the opportunity to witness some of the most famous moments in the legendary club's history. Not every match was won, but behind every occasion lies a story – personal or professional – etched in the memory. And *Anfield South: 75 Years of Liverpool at Wembley* tries to capture those special times – from the famous Wembley pitch to the railway station platform. The sporting 'journey' – and the actual journeys taken by literally hundreds of thousands of supporters – each with their own tale to tell. Another 'day out' at Wembley.

In telling this story I've called upon the support of many individuals. I'll start by thanking the Football Association's Chair, Debbie Hewitt MBE, who has kindly provided the Foreword for the book. Performing her role at the FA with real authority and sincerity, Debbie has seen first-hand how the governing body goes about its huge breadth of work, spends many hours at Wembley Stadium, the organisation's headquarters, and she's a real football fan – and a real Liverpool fan – a genuine supporter. She seemed to be the perfect choice to give the story-telling that lies ahead the right measure of that authority and sincerity – and I'm thrilled to say she was delighted to do just that.

I would especially like to thank those master football statisticians Dave Ball and Ged Rea for their brilliant fact-checking work on every game played by the Reds at both the 'old' and the 'new' Wembley Stadium – and spotting my misplaced passes.

The much-valued Michelle Maple continues to be a huge source of encouragement and support – thanks for being at the end of the phone when my computer skills or, rather, my lack of them stop 'the match' in mid-play.

Paul and Jane Camillin of Pitch Publishing are both great people to deal with – and this is my third book working with them, so we obviously enjoy a good working relationship.

I would like to thank Ivan Butler, Duncan Olner and Graham Hale for their skilled input into editing, cover design and photographic layout respectively. Their work brings the content to life.

At the end of the book, I've included a series of first-hand experiences from Reds' fans who have enjoyed their own big Wembley moment. So, thank you to all of them. I must make special mention of one of those contributors, John Keith, a well-respected journalist, author and broadcaster, who cut his reporting 'teeth' interviewing the great Bill Shankly back in the 1960s.

Over the last seven decades I've collected thousands of programmes, built up scrapbooks, secured some valuable and some offbeat Reds memorabilia and have a library of well over 200 books on or about Liverpool FC and the personalities that have been the living, breathing history of the club. I've dipped into many of those elements to refresh my memory of the many adventures enjoyed by the club and its followers on their frequent visits to Wembley.

I've also found the modern dedicated websites on the club and the sport in general to be another great source of information and research. So thanks to them too.

My own working experiences have given me an incredible insight into how the club has gone about its business and provided me with remarkable access to major moments in their golden history – and I must thank many members of the Anfield 'family' for the help and support down the years.

And my working life at the FA, and at the BBC and ITV has also given me an incredible look 'behind the scenes' on the staging of some of football's biggest matches. So, thank you for all of those priceless opportunities.

Finally, much love and thanks go to my wife, Gerry, for her love, encouragement and patience! We first met back in the early 1980s when we both worked at the BBC – me as producer of *Football Focus*, her as a talented film editor.

And to my sons, Jack and Joe, and our two little grandsons, Monty and Rocco. May they enjoy long and wonderful lives.

And finally, thank you, the reader, for choosing to spend some time in my company. I hope you enjoy the book.

Foreword

I HAD only been in my role as Chair of the Football Association a month when I met Brian Barwick OBE. I had heard about him, of course, so many in sport and nearly all in football have, but there is no substitute for meeting the man himself.

'What can I do to help?' were his first words, and there began a mentorship that has proved and continues to be invaluable to me. What I hadn't appreciated when I first met him was his knowledge, insight and love for Liverpool FC and, as a lifelong Liverpool supporter myself, it is a real privilege to be asked to write this Foreword.

I want to start with his previous books, *Anfield Days and Wembley Ways*, *Watching the Match*, *Sixty Years a Red … and Counting*, and *Sixty Years of the World Cup*. I've read them all. While they cover so many different aspects of the beautiful game, they all have a common theme of a frank, fun and affectionate telling of some of the most powerful football stories of all time. They each reflect Brian's unparalleled experience, the incredible knowledge and behind-the-scenes insight of a broadcaster and journalist, the unique perspective of a former FA Chief Executive and the deep affection of a dedicated football fan.

To anyone who has closely followed Liverpool FC and who has had the privilege of watching many games at Wembley Stadium, this book brings two giants of football together – 'When Liverpool meets Wembley'.

He has written a book that not only captures the legacy of Liverpool and Wembley, but that also has a compelling commentary of defining moments in English history. Whether you are a Liverpool fan, a football fan or a modern historian, this is a gripping tale of a lifetime shaped by the power of the hat-trick of Liverpool, Wembley and football. Through his personal story, Brian explains how the combination of the three has shaped his life, the ups and the downs, the experiences best forgotten and the numerous lessons learned. His writing takes the reader on their own journey – calling out relatable moments that help memories of the path to Wembley and those special Wembley moments come flooding back.

It was some coincidence that my very first FA Cup Final as the Chair of the FA (Saturday, 14 May 2022),was Chelsea vs Liverpool, at Wembley Stadium, of course. I still have Brian's sage advice ahead of the game ringing in my ears, 'Remember the routine … if the Reds score just sit on your hands and look impassively straight ahead.'

It was a 0-0 draw at extra time, which took it to penalties. Liverpool eventually won 6-5. I remembered half of what he said.

Enjoy this fascinating story, written by a great mentor, dear friend and one of the most dedicated football fans I have the privilege of knowing. With Brian's input – I know I need never walk alone.

Debbie Hewitt MBE
FA Chair

Introduction

WHEN I was the Football Association's (FA) CEO, one of the most important roles I had to fulfil was to attend to all the major sporting occasions being staged at Wembley Stadium, and be available to handle any issue, small or large, that required a senior executive response.

On a more emotional and personal note, it meant I would be expected to arrive at Wembley Stadium, now newly rebuilt, several hours before the building would be opened and swiftly packed with up to 90,000 excited football fans, and well before the actual action on the pitch itself got underway.

I always cherished being there super early and, rain or shine, always took the opportunity to walk around the perimeter of the pitch, on my own, several times in an empty stadium. I would suck in that unique atmosphere, the wider sense of stillness and calm, amid the general preparation activities that were happening around me.

Apart from the odd clanking of some metal thing or another, a TV camera being mounted, for example, the cleaning team whistling away as they brushed down each and every seat, or the choirs and armed forces rehearsing their pre-match routines, the stadium, which would later be a cauldron of noise, would be quiet. Very quiet.

As a football lover, first and foremost, I never quite got over the fact that, in a few hours' time, the pitch I was just a few feet away from would host a game of football that would become part of sporting folklore, part of the game's rich heritage and history. Many occasions that before I would have attended as an expectant fan or watched as an avid TV viewer.

But that sense of anticipation was now all around me. You could just feel it in the air. A special moment in time.

What a privilege to have experienced it.

***

It was on 25 April 1914 that Liverpool FC made their debut in the FA Cup Final. A crowd of many thousands from Liverpool itself were packed into the Crystal Palace ground for the Reds' first-ever tilt at cup final glory – their opponents, fellow Lancastrians, Burnley.

Thousands of supporters came down to the capital by train, leaving Friday night or bright and early on Saturday morning. The crowded football specials from Lime Street had excited people on board, cheek by jowl, ready for the adventure of a lifetime.

Every carriage was alive with colour – red and white, of course – badges, ribbons, streamers and rosettes. And many fans sported their freshly minted natty red-and-white bowler hats. Sandwiches, wrapped in red-and-white paper, and the odd bottle of something rather special kept everybody in good spirits.

The roads around the stadium were jam-packed and even the Liverpool team had to use taxis to transport the players from the hotel to the ground. Spectators used every vantage point they could find, including standing on the top of wooden posts and climbing nearby trees, to witness the on-field action.

The game itself was something of a drab affair – a 1-0 win to Burnley – in a stadium that had been named after the dazzling glasshouse that had been built there for the Great

Exhibition of 1851, later transported piece by piece to Hyde Park in central London.

The 1914 FA Cup Final was being held just months before the country would go to war – and for the first time, a reigning monarch, King George V, was in attendance, arriving by chauffeur-driven car to great applause, being introduced to the players before the game and handing the cup over to the triumphant Burnley captain, Tommy Boyle, at the end of the match.

It would be the last time the FA Cup Final would be staged at Crystal Palace – previous locations included the Kennington Oval (the venue of the first FA Cup Final in 1872), Lille Bridge, the Racecourse Ground, Fallowfield Stadium, Goodison Park – and after the conclusion of the First World War, Stamford Bridge.

But, from 1923, football would have its new home, a place and a name that would become synonymous with the sport and its major occasions, a World Cup tournament, European Championships – men's and women's, prestige internationals, European Cup and Champions League finals, FA Cup finals, Football League Cup finals, Premier League matches – the list is endless.

WEMBLEY was to become a name that travelled the world over, essentially for its historic football occasions, but also for an ever-increasing span of other sport and major music events. Wembley, like Wimbledon, Twickenham or Aintree, has become a one-word entry point to big-time sport.

The first recorded mention of one of the world's most iconic sites of sporting and cultural history pops up in AD 757, when Saxon King Offa valued a large spread of green fields and countryside, in what would become better known as north-west London, at just 30 shillings. Offa knew the area as Wemba's Clearing or Wemba's Lea. The world would get to know it more simply as … WEMBLEY.

Built originally as the centrepiece of the British Empire Exhibition of 1924–25, the Empire Stadium, Wembley, was built in just 300 days at a cost of £750,000, a phenomenal achievement in itself. King George VI cut the first sod at Wembley – and later became one of the stadium's most honoured visitors.

Legend has it that the famous lush pitch was part constructed with turf lifted from the putting greens that had been a feature of the golf course that originally occupied the site of the great Wembley exhibition.

The Empire Stadium held the world's largest gathering of scouts, a rodeo, a pageant and choir among the Exhibition's events, but at one point, subsequent to the end of those celebrations, it was seen as something of a 'white elephant'.

Indeed, it was nearly lost to the nation, but having hosted its first FA Cup Final in 1923, and its first international between England and Scotland a year later, football, and possibly the FA's desire to give the FA Cup Final a permanent home, gave it a fighting chance of having a successful future.

And the rest is history. And a spectacular one. The late, great Billy Wright, who made 105 appearances for England, a record 90 of them as captain, in the 1950s, said this: 'How does it feel when you lead a team out of the tunnel at Wembley Stadium? I can only describe it as if you have stepped into another world.'

As well as becoming 'the home' of English football, including the never-to-be-forgotten 1966 World Cup Final, the stadium has played host to a remarkable list of other sports, firstly under the Twin Towers, and latterly under the Arch, including: greyhound racing, speedway, world championship boxing, rugby league and rugby union, American football, baseball, motorsport, show-jumping, athletics, hockey, wrestling … and even ski jumping!

The stadium was also the centrepiece of the 1948 Olympic Games, a celebration of peace and a symbol of how sport could help reunite a world so badly damaged by the war that had preceded it.

Over the years, the stadium also became a must-play venue for the world's premier rock and pop stars – and it most memorably hosted the Live Aid Concert on 13 July 1985. Pop 'royalty' was on show that day at an event inspired and driven by Bob Geldof, raising £70 million for starving families in Africa. On other occasions, His Holiness Pope John Paul II and world-famous evangelist Billy Graham would preach in front of thousands at the stadium.

And daredevil American motorbike rider Evel Knievel realised himself that there was a difference between heaven and hell when his failed attempt at clearing 13 single-decker buses on his two-wheeler ended with him breaking his pelvis in front of 90,000 spectators. Despite the crash, the irrepressible Knievel refused a stretcher, instead walking off the hallowed Wembley turf, stating, 'I came in walking, I went out walking!'

A genuine piece of sporting history – the 1923 FA Cup Final between Bolton Wanderers and West Ham United – was the first football match played at the stadium. It will always be remembered as the 'White Horse Final' as a photographer captured an enduring black-and-white image of PC George Scorey, astride Billy, trying with his colleagues – both human and equine – to control a crowd well in excess of its expected capacity of 120,000.

No accurate crowd figure can be established for that opening event, but an exaggerated legend has it that more than 250,000 people swarmed into the stadium that day. The final's kick-off was put back 45 minutes as the crowd was edged back behind the touchlines – and the first goal at Wembley Stadium came just two minutes into the game,

David Jack scoring the opener for Bolton in their 2-0 victory over the Hammers.

Ten years later, Everton, and their famous centre-forward Dixie Dean, would beat Manchester City 3-0, at Wembley, their second FA Cup Final victory in their fifth appearance in the climax of the competition. Everton fans made the most of the fact that their near-neighbours and closest rivals, Liverpool, still hadn't won the most famous cup competition in world football – or, indeed, stepped on the most revered stretch of grass in sport.

All that was to change in due course, but it wasn't until 1950 that Liverpool finally made their debut, albeit at a rainy Wembley Stadium. It was the first of nearly 50 appearances there for Liverpool over the next 75 years – a remarkable journey, abounding with many great wins, some fantastic stories and the odd tough-to-take defeat.

Liverpool and Wembley have become regular bed-fellows – to such a degree that Scousers, of the red persuasion, gave the national stadium a brand-new name: ANFIELD SOUTH! And those legions of Liverpool fans have travelled down in their thousands time and again to witness their heroes compete for silverware in the world's most famous stadium.

Of course, Anfield will always be the club's truly iconic home, but Wembley has staged many of their most famous moments too. And in surroundings that are guaranteed to capture the world's attention. The late, great Pelé summed it up beautifully: 'Wembley is the cathedral. It is the capital of football, and it is the heart of football.'

And Liverpool Football Club and its army of fans would spend many red-letter days there.

Chapter 1

1950s: Liddellpool's Wembley Damp Debut!

AS THE country entered a new post-war decade, the after-effects of six years of traumatic conflict still hung heavily over the nation's population.

Times were tough, families were still mourning the tragic loss of loved ones, rationing was slowly being phased out but was still holding back choice and quantity, and people were struggling to settle back into their old way of life.

In February 1950, Labour, under Clement Attlee, won a second term of government but with a slim majority of just five seats – in stark contrast to the 146-seat majority that he gained previously. A clear sign of the public's disaffection with how things were going.

On a lighter note, the new decade was about to launch some cultural innovations that would go some way to giving people a route back to normality. On BBC Radio, such an important element of British social life back then, *Educating Archie*, the adventures of a naughty young schoolboy – incredibly, a ventriloquist's dummy(!) – became a smash hit and gave some upcoming stars, like future comic genius Tony Hancock, a chance to shine. In 1950, BBC Radio also ran a pilot episode of an agricultural soap opera, *The Archers*. The series proper began the following year and still has a following in its millions to this day.

The Eagle comic first appeared, featuring Dan Dare and Captain Pugwash, and the first broadcast of the popular pre-school children's programme *Andy Pandy* enchanted youngsters for many decades that followed – including this author! Pantomimes popped up all over the country and, in Liverpool, well-loved comedian Frankie Howerd starred as Simple Simon in *Puss in Boots*.

Meanwhile, at the busy Liverpool docks, the Overhead Railway, first installed in 1893 and the world's first electrically operated railway, was still in operation before being closed later in the decade.

In sport, the first Formula 1 Grand Prix was held at Silverstone. Freebooter would win the Grand National, and in June the first World Cup since 1938 was staged in Brazil – the hosts ultimately beaten by Uruguay in the final. The England national team competed for the first time – and they suffered a humiliating loss to the United States in Belo Horizonte en route to an early exit from the competition.

Football in England had got back underway in 1945/46, with a truncated league programme and an FA Cup competition won by Derby County in a 4-1 win over Charlton Athletic.

In the first full season after the end of the war, Liverpool won the First Division title for the fifth time, the previous successes being in 1900/01, 1905/06, 1921/22 and 1922/23. In a tight finish, Liverpool headed Manchester United and Wolverhampton Wanderers, and were under the control of ex-West Ham United defender George Kay, who had captained the London side in the famous 1923 FA Cup Final. 'He was the Shankly of his day. He ate, slept and lived for one thing only – football,' Reds forward Cyril Done opined on his boss.

Kay's total commitment to the cause also led him down a path of ill health. He was respected by his players and his managerial peers as a man who embraced innovation and portrayed a refreshing humane side to his nature. He had been open to ideas like taking his team over to the USA during the close season in 1946 to make sure they were able to eat nourishing food, including huge steaks, maple syrup and fresh orange juice, ahead of a long league campaign in still-rationed England.

Liverpool's final game of the 1946/47 season at Molineux was a 2-1 win for the Reds, but their championship win wasn't secured until a fortnight later when Sheffield United's win over Stoke City confirmed Liverpool's place at the top of the First Division. It could have been the double for the Reds that season because they reached the semi-final of the FA Cup before going out in a replay to Burnley.

Five league titles but no FA Cup. Back then, the FA Cup Final was still the biggest deal – the one football match that brought the whole nation together. And Liverpool were about to have another chance of winning it – and with their star player leading the charge.

Billy Liddell is a genuine all-time Liverpool great. He sits comfortably alongside the likes of Sir Kenny Dalglish and Steven Gerrard. And it is only the fact that he played his football over 70 years ago – and footage of his remarkable ability is sparse and that many who enjoyed watching him are no longer with us – that probably denies him the completely comparative level of respect. I started watching Liverpool in the 1961/62 season – one year after Billy played his final game for the Reds – completing an outstanding record of 534 games and 228 goals. Those statistics only tell half of the story.

Born in Dunfermline in Scotland, Liddell played for the Fifeshire junior club, Lochgelly Violet, before signing for Liverpool in 1939, only for the war to prevent him taking his place in the First Division. Liddell played in most of the Regional League matches during the early 1940s before joining the RAF, serving in Europe and Canada, and turning out for its wartime team, Bomber Command.

He was demobbed just a few weeks into the 1946/47 season and made 34 appearances for a Liverpool team that went on to lift the championship. He was a winger who could play on either flank or lead the line as a free-scoring centre-forward or inside-forward. He even shored up the defence during one stint as a full-back. Such was his influence on his team-mates and the club's performances that the side was soon being dubbed 'Liddellpool'. He carried the side through a disappointing period in the 1950s, which included a stint in the Second Division. And the Kop loved him for it. As did his team-mates.

'Billy was so strong he was unbelievable,' said the late Bob Paisley. 'He would always battle, challenge and show tenacity.' Fellow Liverpool legend Ian Callaghan who made his debut in place of his boyhood hero, Billy Liddell, said, 'When I was a youngster Billy was my hero. I was just so absolutely impressed by him ... by his speed and how hard he hit a ball. Dear me! He looked so big, and he had a pair of legs on him like I don't know what!'

A proud Scotsman with nearly 30 caps, Liddell was recognised as an awesome talent. When the selectors chose their Great Britain representative sides against the Rest of Europe in front of 137,000 spectators at Hampden Park in 1947, and in Belfast in 1955, he was one of only two men to be included in both line-ups. The other? Stanley Matthews. That past master of the written word, Geoffrey Green, described Liddell thus: 'Billy Liddell was the greatest gentleman the game has ever known.'

Billy Liddell, 'Our Billy' as the Kop would chant, was a truly special player and a truly special person. Amazingly, he put together a remarkable career that, because of his part-time accountancy job, was restricted to him being able to train only twice a week! In 1950, Billy and his Liverpool team-mates had their eyes on the big prize, the FA Cup, and a trip to Wembley Stadium.

Liverpool's FA Cup journey started with a third-round replay over Blackburn Rovers, then they disposed of Exeter City, though not without a struggle. A tough fifth-round tie at Stockport County was won by the odd goal of three, and Blackpool were beaten at Anfield in the competition's quarter-final.

Everton had also progressed to the last four, as had Chelsea and Arsenal. Potential for the first all-Merseyside FA Cup Final were dashed when the near-neighbours were drawn together. The semi-final took place at Maine Road on the same Saturday as the Grand National at Aintree. It was only the second time the two senior Merseyside clubs had met at the penultimate stage of the FA Cup, the previous occasion being in 1906, when Everton won and went on to win the final itself.

As Freebooter won the nation's favourite horse race, Liverpool took the honours at Maine Road in front of over 72,000 fans, with goals from wing-half Bob Paisley and a 62nd-minute clincher from Billy Liddell. Liverpool fans were cock-a-hoop and, in author Peter Kenny Jones's fascinating book on *Liddell at One Hundred*, he revived a song sung by the Reds' fans to the tune of '(Put Another Nickel In) Music, Music, Music'.

Put another record on, Liverpool two and
Everton none,
All we want is a cup final to Wembley
Wembley, Wembley,
Albert scoring goals galore,
Billy Liddell scoring more,

All we want is a cup final ticket to Wembley
Wembley, Wembley.
When we all go to Wembley,
You'll find the Everton team turning green, with
Envy that cannot be seen,
So, give three cheers for the good old reds,
They made the blues forget their heads.
We will bring the cup home soon from Wembley,
Wembley, Wembley.

Liverpool's semi-final win set up an FA Cup Final against Arsenal, who had beaten Chelsea after a replay – and Liverpool were entitled to feel confident about the forthcoming tussle, having won both of that season's league encounters against the Gunners – 2-0 at Anfield, with a brace of Liddell goals, and 2-1 at Highbury through two goals from Albert Stubbins. In the five-week gap between the semi-finals and the FA Cup Final itself, both teams' league form tapered off, as was often the case.

One oddity in the build-up to the final was that the Arsenal captain, Joe Mercer, was allowed to train at Melwood, Liverpool's training ground. Mercer lived on the Wirral and was a well-loved football figure. He gained permission to train in the afternoon after the Liverpool players had gone through their paces in the morning.

The countdown to the 1950 FA Cup Final was underway.

* * *

It is perhaps difficult for the younger generation to fully grasp the historic importance of the FA Cup as a competition, and the FA Cup Final itself as one of the most engaging and exciting highlights in the sporting calendar – the unpredictability of the early rounds, coupled with the potential of giant-killing acts by the smaller clubs, and the replays, played within a few days of the original ties having been played.

Even the cup draw itself had radio listeners on the edge of their armchairs, as the FA bigwigs put the 'balls into the velvet bag', gave them a good shake and then pulled them out one by one to create the next round of matches in the FA Cup. It was magical stuff.

Remember, in 1950 there was the established football league programme, the First Division, the Second Division and the Third Division (North and South). There was no second professional domestic cup competition and no European football competitions.

The status of the FA Cup has been 'bumped and bashed' about in recent times – partly to help squeeze more matches from Europe's club competitions into an already hectic fixture schedule and to facilitate more international football. But let's take a trip back in time and see how the nation, relishing a little more normality in their post-war lives, were able to get their FA Cup Final 'fix' at the start of the 1950s.

The BBC first showed the FA Cup Final on its fledging television service in 1938 when Preston North End, with wing-half and future Liverpool legend Bill Shankly in their ranks, beat Huddersfield Town 1-0 with a last-minute penalty in extra time. There were only 10,000 TV sets in the country at that time, and radio would remain the senior service for two more decades.

In the 1949/50 season, the BBC TV's grandly named 'Association Football' coverage amounted to just 14 live matches – ten matches from the Isthmian League, an England vs Italy international from Tottenham and, on the preceding Saturdays before the Arsenal vs Liverpool FA Cup Final clash, a Schoolboy International between England and Scotland, and the FA Amateur Cup Final between Bishop Auckland and Willington.

It was the 1950 FA Cup Final that started the ball rolling in terms of what was the relative worth of a big live football match with its national appeal. The facility fee paid by the BBC to the FA in respect of the 1950 FA Cup Final was little more than the princely sum of £262!

The Arsenal vs Liverpool match – north vs south – pulled an estimated television audience of one million viewers from the 350,000 homes now having a TV set to watch it on. The sets themselves had a tiny screen on which to carry the pictures. The many more without a TV set had to be more inventive – that included the late and great BBC commentator John Motson: 'My father was a Methodist minister and, when I was five years old, he took me to a musical instrument shop in Woolwich called Drysdales. They had a nine-inch TV in a backstairs room and that's where I watched the 1950 FA Cup Final.'

There was a full league programme on the day of the final, and poor attendances at first-class matches played that afternoon in the London and Birmingham area – the two regions carrying television pictures from Wembley – set a hare running. London's first-class match attendances were down 42 per cent and Birmingham's by 39 per cent.

In 1951, to try to stem the flow of would-be spectators turning into TV viewers, only the second half of the cup final was allowed to be shown live, but by 1953 the BBC was paying a £1,000 facility fee for full live match coverage, and the FA Cup Final stood alone in the fixture list. Even on football's big day back in 1950, the game had no monopoly on screen time, as one of the BBC's famous continuity presenters, Mary Malcolm, elegantly dressed, eloquently underlined just an hour before the big kick-off of Arsenal vs Liverpool:

> Good afternoon. Today is cup final day, and, of course, the weather is just about as bad as it could

> be. It's been raining hard all morning but in spite of everything, enthusiasm is running high as ever at Wembley.
>
> We'll be taking you there to join the community singing ... but for now, until 2.30 Frances Perry and Fred Streeter are going to give you some hints on gardening ... First then, here is Frances Perry to talk about chrysanthemums.

Just your average FA Cup Final build-up!

On BBC Radio's Light Programme, coverage also started at 2.30pm, after an hour's worth of commentary from the MCC vs Yorkshire cricket match, followed by 30 minutes of music from the BBC's Northern Ireland Light Orchestra. Radio commentary for the big game came from the famous voices of Raymond Glendenning and Alan Clarke, with summaries from Charles Buchan and Henry Rose.

Watching it on this new-fangled TV thing or listening to it on the more familiar and respected 'sound radio', still nothing beats being at the game itself! And that privilege was afforded to a meagre 8,000 Liverpool fans – the lucky ones from the 100,000 ticket applications received by the Anfield club.

To manage expectation, the club's response to such a paltry allocation of tickets was to make the ballot for these prized possessions only open to people living within 25 miles of the city. As I write, I have in front of me a used ticket from the match and if you were sitting in Wembley's North Terrace in Row 28 Seat 310, it had cost you 7s/6d in 'old money'.

***

When asked about the most thrilling experience of his life in *Liverpool FC Wembley 1950 Players' Souvenir Brochure*, wing-half Bob Paisley would have wrong-footed everybody with his answer. 'It has nothing to do with football,' he said, 'it was the unforgettable sight of Mount Vesuvius in eruption while stationed near Naples during the war.'

On the eve of the 1950 FA Cup Final, it was Paisley who was blowing his own top when he was controversially left out of the Liverpool team to play at Wembley, despite playing in every round up to the climax, including scoring a key goal in the semi-final. Paisley had already been a member of the Bishop Auckland side who won the 1939 FA Amateur Cup Final against Willington at Roker Park. After that match was finished, his team-mate, Laurie Wensley, who had scored a hat-trick, used the boardroom table on which to sign a contract with Sunderland – at the other end of the club's polished table a 20-year-old Bob Paisley signed as a professional for Liverpool. Bob received a £10 signing-on fee, and his weekly pay was to be £5.

Before the year was out, the Second World War was underway, delaying Paisley's Liverpool league debut until 1946, robbing him and many of his contemporaries of a huge slice of their professional careers. Paisley was called up in October 1939 and joined the 73rd Regiment of the Royal Artillery. He would go on to serve in Montgomery's Eighth Army, the Desert Rats and, in 1944, when the Allies liberated Rome, Bob, with his fellow soldiers, travelled through the Eternal City aboard a tank, to the delight of the joyful civilians.

Thirty-three years later, Paisley would enjoy another major moment of his life in Rome as manager of a Liverpool team winning the European Cup for the first time. Post-war, and a title winner in 1946/47, Paisley had established himself as a hard-working, hard-tackling wing-half and had made over 125 league appearances as the club prepared for their big day at Wembley. A knee injury had prevented Paisley playing in the four league games leading up to the final but he was fit and available to play at Wembley.

George Kay, the manager, did not pick the Liverpool team for the final; it was the nine club directors who, by a slim 5-4 majority, chose Bill Jones over Paisley in the left-half berth. It was left to the manager to break the news to the heartbroken Paisley.

Paisley's name might have been in the FA Cup Final programme team line-up, but he never set foot on the pitch. Bob Paisley was devastated by the decision: 'It hit me so hard in 1950 that if a club had come in for me, and Liverpool had wanted me to go, then I would have left. But during the summer I thought about it and concluded that even if I had left, the same thing could happen somewhere else.'

Ironically, Paisley was chosen to play in Liverpool's final league game just four days after the final – and played 41 league games the following season. He retired in 1954, having played 277 games for the Merseyside club. He joined the backroom staff en route to becoming the most successful manager in British football history.

***

Liverpool manager George Kay had served in the Royal Garrison Artillery in the First World War. That sense of military duty came to the fore as, when the Second World War broke out, he persuaded the whole of his Liverpool team to sign on for the Territorial Army. So, less than a week after playing football in that season's First Division, most Liverpool players found themselves in a different type of uniform, guarding the Mersey Tunnel!

On another occasion, Kay also had an unusual brush with a British military great, Field Marshal Montgomery of Alamein. Liverpool were playing Portsmouth at Fratton Park and George, not one to mince his words, was getting so carried away on the touchline that 'Monty', then Pompey's president, sent a policeman down to ask the Reds' boss to curb his language. You couldn't argue with that. But George Kay did. He went round to see Monty after the game, they settled their differences, before getting on like a house on fire when discovering they were both socialists.

Sadly, in April 1950, on the way down from Liverpool to their pre-cup final headquarters, George Kay took ill and stayed in his hotel bed until the morning of the game. He insisted that he wouldn't miss Wembley, but he was far from well once there. The weeks building up to the final had taken their toll on the Liverpool boss, including the last few days of intense nervous strain before Liverpool's big day. He would resign as Liverpool manager a year later and died in April 1954.

Billy Liddell said: 'If ever a man gave his life for a club, George Kay did so for Liverpool.'

* * *

So to the 1950 FA Cup Final itself. As the BBC's Mary Malcolm had made clear, the big day arrived at the same time as a bout of heavy persistent rain. Twenty-four hours earlier, when the Liverpool players had visited an empty Wembley Stadium to get a feel of the famous venue, the sun had been beating down. The players had checked where their respective families would be sitting – out in the open about ten rows from the front. Perfect … unless it rained the following afternoon that is.

As both teams' primary colours were red, the teams were asked to change. Liverpool would be playing in white shirts and black shorts and had worn those colours the previous weekend at Portsmouth, to get used to their change of strip. Arsenal wore old gold shirts with white shorts. Their line-up included the two Compton brothers, Les and the flamboyant Denis. The latter was to become a cricketing legend, while his football career came to an end through serious knee damage.

On the big day, he countered the cold and wet conditions at Wembley by knocking back a large brandy at half-time.

Pre-match, both teams had been presented to the royal guest of honour, King George VI, and, formalities over, Liverpool skipper Phil Taylor won the toss. Arsenal didn't waste any time in trying to close down the threat of the Reds' superstar, Billy Liddell. As one writer observed: 'He, Herculean in endeavour, was surrounded wherever and whenever in possession and on one occasion it took four men to prevent his escapes.'

One Arsenal player who knew first-hand the potency of Liddell was his fellow Scottish international team-mate Alex Forbes. He frequently fouled Liddell, man-marking him and obstructing him whenever possible. Much was made of Forbes's malevolent treatment of 'Our Billy', including a significantly high tackle but, after the game, Liddell typically made light of it: 'Far be it from me to impute any malicious motives to Alex. I'm absolutely sure he had none. We'd played together for Scotland and always got on extremely well.'

Arsenal won the match 2-0, both goals scored by Reg Lewis, one in each half. The official attendance for the final was 100,000 and the gate receipts £39,296. Reds full-back Ray Lambert said, 'When Lewis scored the Arsenal goals that beat us, we had defensive gaps that looked on the Wembley pitch as wide as the Mersey Tunnel.'

The newspaper headlines that evening summed it up: 'Arsenal, Well-Used to Wembley Air, Bore Too Much Power For Anfield Side'; 'FA Cup Still Eludes Liverpool After 58 Years' Play'.

Saturday evening was spent in London at a post-match banquet but there was one VIP missing – the FA Cup itself. And, perhaps a quaint reflection of the times, the Liverpool team and associates went on a coach trip to the seaside at Brighton on the Sunday.

On the Monday, they received a heroes' welcome back after arriving at Lime Street Station, welcomed by tens of thousands lining the streets, before heading off to Anfield, where a junior match was in progress. A crowd of around 30,000 gave the players and officials a fantastic reception. Then, it was to the town hall, where another 10,000 people heralded their favourites.

Billy Liddell was genuinely moved: 'Even the most hardened members of our party were really touched by this amazing expression of loyalty. All in all, it was an unforgettable and moving homecoming after the disappointment of losing at Wembley.'

And the FA Cup itself did make it to Merseyside after all, brought by Arsenal captain Joe Mercer and displayed in his family's grocery business in Wallasey!

Added Time:

- The Reds were relegated from the First Division in 1954. Everton were promoted in the same season from the Second Division. Kop favourite Albert Stubbins would leave Anfield in 1953 but was guaranteed legendary status for being chosen as one of the famous faces on the cover of the Beatles' iconic *Sgt. Pepper's Lonely Hearts Club Band* album.
- Liverpool's record defeat is 9-1 – conceded against Birmingham City in December 1954. They suffered their most famous embarrassing loss in the FA Cup third round in January 1959 – 2-1 against non-league Worcester City. Billy Liddell remained the Kop's 'main man' throughout the decade.
- In December 1959, Bill Shankly joined the Anfield club to turn the club's miserable 50s record around – and the rest is history.

Chapter 2

1960s: And the Queen Wore Red!

The noisiest, most one-sided Cup Final Wembley has ever seen, wrote a new glittering page in the history of Liverpool Football Club, for here was their first triumph in more than seventy years of endeavour. No wonder that on Saturday night, the toast was, 'at last'.

That Liverpool won worthily and well is beyond question. If ever there was a two-horse race with one left at the winning post, this was it.

Here was a day Liverpool's vast football public, whether fortunate enough to be inside the stadium or at home in front of their television sets, will never forget. After so much unrewarding wandering in a wilderness reserved for FA Cup also-rans. Here was that wonderful break-through – the triumph of triumphs.

– Horace Yates, *Liverpool Daily Post*, 3 May 1965

Winning the FA Cup for the first time in the club's history, ending a 73-year wait, was a great relief. I can tell you. It was a terrible thing for the club to have gone that long without winning it. There are all sorts of stories that if Liverpool did win it, the Liver Birds would leave the Pier Head.

– Bill Shankly

> Wembley Stadium – that's the place every player dreams about. FA Cup Final day is something apart from every other day in your career. The final has such a tradition, such a place in soccer history, that it was always the No.1 ambition for me. On 1 May 1965, I achieved it at Wembley … and that's still the biggest thrill of my soccer life. Yes, even greater than winning the World Cup.
>
> – Roger Hunt

> The ball came to me perfectly, straight to my head, and that was it. I couldn't miss. The goal yawned at me as big as the Mersey Tunnel. I saw it nestling in the back of the net and was overcome with emotion. The cup was ours!
>
> – Ian St John

> Ee-Aye-Addio, we've won the cup!
>
> – The fans

Saturday, 1 May 1965 was indeed a red-letter day for Liverpool Football Club. Their increasingly desperate annual pursuit to win the world's greatest domestic cup competition was finally over. The Reds' second trip to the iconic Wembley Stadium had ended with a glorious 2-1 victory over Leeds United – after extra time – with goals from Roger Hunt and Ian St John, and the Liverpool fans making a noise the likes of which had never been heard before under the Twin Towers.

Their singing, chanting and full-on fervour made the occasion even more special – the stadium, or the Liverpool end at least, was absolutely rocking. As was the city of Liverpool, or at least half of it! What a day, what a weekend – all those years ago.

***

> The Fifties were in black and white; the Sixties burst into glorious technicolour
>
> – Anon

The 1960s will always be remembered, by those of us still around to have lived through them, as a period when the nation kickstarted itself from the austerity of the previous decade and began to live a little. Rationing was over, conscription had ended, the 'pill' was introduced, colour television was beamed into people's homes, Carnaby Street became as recognisable a London address as Downing Street – another street, TV's *Coronation Street*, began its long and extraordinarily popular life, and the miniskirt became an iconic look. Ordinary working people had more disposable income than their predecessors, and there was a greater sense of optimism and fun around the place.

London, the home of Wembley Stadium, was deemed the capital of the country's 'Swinging Sixties'. The capital of the decade's '*Singing* Sixties' was much further north. Liverpool, to be exact. The whole of Liverpool came alive in the 1960s – The Beatles conquered the world with pop music that still feels as fresh today as it did all that time ago. The 'Fab Four' created memories with each new single and LP released, eagerly awaited by their legion of adoring fans. 'Beatlemania' was born.

'Merseybeat' was alive and well and, under the shrewd management of Brian Epstein, The Beatles were feted on both sides of the Atlantic, having just released their second feature film *Help*. Epstein's other groups, such as Gerry and the Pacemakers, The Fourmost, and Billy J. Kramer and the Dakotas, also enjoyed huge success, as did many other local Liverpool bands, and a young lady, a cloakroom attendant at

The Cavern, Cilla Black, would stop hanging coats up and sing her way into people's hearts and the top of the charts, en route to becoming a 'national treasure'.

Gerry and the Pacemakers' version of 'You'll Never Walk Alone' became their third successive number one in the 1963 pop charts – but this rendition of the Rodgers and Hammerstein song was to enjoy a much longer life. The late Gerry Marsden reflected on its phenomenal success:

> It really was the strength of the words that attracted me to 'You'll Never Walk Alone'. I first heard it when I went to the cinema to see the musical *Carousel* – the melody was beautiful, the dramatic effect strong and I immediately loved the sentiment of the message. A few weeks after I'd recorded it in 1963, it was sung by the crowd at Anfield. And through the years, Liverpool Football Club and I have been strongly linked because the song has been adopted as their anthem.

The city's rich vein of comedy and its citizens' razor-sharp wit was given huge profile with the likes of Ken Dodd and Jimmy Tarbuck enjoying major success on TV, radio and stage. It wasn't just in the field of music and entertainment that the city of Liverpool was making strides. Its two big Merseyside football clubs, Liverpool and Everton, were on a run of great form and enjoying significant achievement.

Bill Shankly had arrived like a whirlwind at Anfield in December 1959, and his unique style of management – ambitious, driven, determined and single-minded – turned a football club that was enduring a series of near misses in getting out of the Second Division into a team that got promoted, won the league championship twice and the FA Cup once, all in the space of five seasons.

His pursuit and purchase of fellow Scotsmen Ron Yeats and Ian St John in 1961 was game-changing. The later acquisition of Preston's talented winger Peter Thompson, in 1963, joining the ranks of brilliant goal-getter Roger Hunt, local Liverpool lads like Ian Callaghan, Gerry Byrne, Chris Lawler, Ronnie Moran and Tommy Smith, a rock-solid goalkeeper in Tommy Lawrence, and astute signings of Gordon Milne, Willie Stevenson and Geoff Strong made Liverpool a force to be reckoned with both in England and across Europe.

As well as winning league titles in 1963/64 and 1965/66, Shankly's men went close to reaching the 1963 FA Cup Final before losing to their bogey team Leicester City in the semi-final at Hillsborough. Liverpool's undeserved 1-0 defeat that afternoon would be reversed en route to their own 1965 FA Cup Final.

Their journey to Wembley in 1965 took various twists and turns. The Reds squeezed through their third-round tie at West Bromwich Albion, before drawing at home 1-1 against Stockport County, then lying 92nd and bottom of the whole Football League. Earlier in the day the nation had come to a halt to mark the funeral of Sir Winston Churchill.

Bill Shankly, on a scouting mission in Germany to watch European Cup opponents Cologne, almost choked on his duty-free when he was told the result. And the plucky County hit the underside of the bar in the last minute. Shankly arrived back in the country after his scouting mission and asked an airport porter, 'Any surprises in the FA Cup today?'

'No, not really,' came the reply. 'Oh, Stockport drew 1-1 with Liverpool at Anfield.' Shankly was staggered. 'Christ, son … and you don't think that was a f*****g surprise!' In front of a replay crowd of over 24,000 at Stockport, Liverpool, this time in front of their manager, Bill Shankly, put the tie to bed 2-0.

Bolton Wanderers away was the Reds' fifth-round tie, and a rare headed goal by winger Ian Callaghan, late in the game, was the decisive moment. The Reds' quarter-final tie paired them with Leicester City, the team that had broken their hearts in the semi-final two years before. Indeed, since being promoted back into the First Division and ahead of their quarter-final clash, Liverpool had played Leicester City seven times in league and cup matches and won only once. A 0-0 draw at Filbert Street was followed by a 1-0 win for Liverpool in the replay, a Roger Hunt goal, in front of over 53,000, doing the business for the Reds.

As well as now reaching the FA Cup semi-final, Shankly's men had reached the semi-final of the European Cup – at their first attempt. The opening tie back in August had been against Icelandic no-hopers Reykjavík, winning the away leg 5-0 and the home leg 6-1.

Next up were the Belgian champions, Anderlecht, a team Bill Shankly had lots of respect for, and he made a sartorial change for his players for the home leg. Liverpool played in their all-red kit for the first time. Stylish football matched a stylish new kit and Liverpool won a convincing 3-0 in front of an adoring Anfield crowd. A Roger Hunt goal secured a 1-0 win in Belgium.

Back in European Cup quarter-final action in February, Cologne and Liverpool shared a goalless draw in Germany. Controversially, the second leg at a snow-bound Anfield was called off shortly before the kick-off, much to the annoyance of the Cologne officials and players. When the game was eventually staged a fortnight later, a virtuoso performance by Cologne's goalkeeper, Toni Schumacher, kept the Reds at bay and another 0-0 draw was the result. A decider took place in Rotterdam, which ended 2-2 after extra time – the Reds having led 2-0 at one stage of the match.

This was the famous occasion when Liverpool went through to the European Cup semi-final, and a two-legged tie against holders Inter Milan, on the toss of a small wooden disc – red on one side and white on the other. The first time the referee tossed the disc up in the air, it got stuck in the churned-up mud on the pitch – so the ref tossed it up again and, this time, it clearly landed red side up – and a jubilant Liverpool captain Ron Yeats later explained: 'I swear I jumped six feet in the air. The rest of the players saw me jump and knew we were through.'

Just three days later, the Reds met a very talented Chelsea side in an FA Cup semi-final at Villa Park. And despite their exertions in the Netherlands, Shankly's men beat the London side 2-0, with goals from Peter Thompson and a penalty from Willie Stevenson – the first he had ever taken! The raw memories of their semi-final defeat against Leicester City two years before were finally put to bed – Liverpool were in the 1965 FA Cup Final.

And a very special day at Wembley Stadium awaited them.

* * *

In our family home in Childwall, Liverpool, there was a real sense of excitement, anticipation and a whole ton of nerves.

Saturday, 1 May 1965 had finally arrived – FA Cup Final day. And it wasn't just any old cup final day – this one was for us, for real – Liverpool vs Leeds United. I had my first taste of watching FA Cup finals live on the telly in 1962 – Tottenham Hotspur vs Burnley; in 1963 Manchester United played Leicester City, and in 1964 West Ham United grabbed a last-gasp winner against Preston North End. But for the 1965 FA Cup Final, as a ten-year-old schoolboy, I had planned the big day down to the last throw-in.

> 8.30am: breakfast – snap, crackle and pop – a bowl of Rice Krispies – and two pieces of toast with strawberry jam (… following a sleepless night).
>
> 10.00am: a quick walk up to the 'top shops' to get my supplies in for the long day ahead – a couple of packets of Opal Fruits, a tube of Polo mints, a quarter-pound's worth of Maynard's Wine Gums, a box of Liquorice Allsorts – and a large bottle of Tizer.
>
> 10.30am: final read-through of all the various souvenir papers – Liverpool Yeah, Yeah, Yeah!, purchased with my pocket money over the previous week. And then a quick flick through the *Radio Times*, which splashed its coverage of the FA Cup Final all over its front cover, with rosettes of both competing clubs.
>
> 11.25am: 'bag' the armchair nearest our black-and-white television set.
>
> 11.30am: the opening credits roll and that famous signature tune blasts out for BBC's FA Cup Final *Grandstand* introduced by David Coleman – the go-to man for the big occasion. Curtains drawn, armchair secured, sweets and lemonade at the ready – and the next six hours sorted.

BBC's *Cup Final Grandstand* – a ritual in homes all over the country – with all the familiar ingredients: 'Meet the Teams'; 'How They Got There'; the story of that year's FA Cup competition; interviews with the two managers live from the team hotels; celebrity fans of both clubs; the players boarding the coach en route, from the gentle atmosphere created by the well-wishing locals outside their 'hideaway hotel', grabbing some late autographs, to the complete mayhem and madness of Wembley on cup final day; pre-match pitch-side chats with that afternoon's stars; the community singing led by Frank Rea; the teams walking out to an explosion of crowd noise and meeting that afternoon's dignitaries; and finally the big match itself.

The FA Cup Final is underway, followed by the presentation of the FA Cup itself to the winning captain, having climbed those 39 steps from the pitch to the Royal Box, the winning team's glorious lap of honour, and the interviews with the triumphant captain and his team's man of the match – with the trophy, of course.

Closing titles sequence … on with BBC1's Saturday evening fare, including *Juke Box Jury*, *Dr Who* and *The Dick Van Dyke Show*. Me and my mates would be outdoors replaying the game on a small strip of grass at the end of our road – which doubled for Wimbledon, Lord's or Wembley, as the sporting calendar demanded.

***

Amazingly, Liverpool had to play *ten* league games in April to complete their league season – ten matches in 26 days. No large squads, remember, and no substitutes – Liverpool's recognised 'starting XI' played in most of the matches, with a sprinkling of appearances of reserve players drafted in to fill the odd gap. Imagine how Jürgen Klopp would have responded to that fixture backlog!

It was only on the Monday before the following Saturday's cup final that Shankly picked a largely reserve side for their final league match of the season at Wolverhampton:

> Molyneux; Lowry, Moran; Hignett, Ferns, Strong; Graham, Arrowsmith, Sealey, Chisnall, Wallace.

Only Geoff Strong from those 11 chosen to play Wolves would feature in the FA Cup Final – mind you, Shankly's shadow squad won 3-1 to help the Reds finish seventh in the league. Strong had started the season as an Arsenal player and actually scored against Liverpool at Anfield on the opening day of the season – it was the match that was featured on the first-ever edition of BBC's *Match of the Day*, in August 1964. He made it into Liverpool's cup final line-up in place of the Reds' international half-back, Gordon Milne, who was injured in a league match at Chelsea just a fortnight before the big match at Wembley. His knee ligaments badly damaged, Milne knew he was out of the final whatever anybody said to make him feel better.

The Liverpool team travelled from Lime Street Station to Euston Station, where they were then picked up by a coach to complete their journey to their pre-cup final hotel in leafy Weybridge. On the eve of the final, the Liverpool party travelled back into the capital to see the first house of Ken Dodd's long-running smash-hit show *Doddy's Here* at the London Palladium. Ken Dodd, a hero on Merseyside, was more than just a comic maestro – he could sing a bit as well. And, in 1965, his recording of an old Italian ballad 'Tears' sold over a million copies and spent 24 weeks in the charts – five of them at number one – and ended up the best-selling single of the year, the third-biggest-selling single of the 1960s, and it was the only non-Beatles song in the top five.

Doddy was a keen Liverpool fan and during the show he got the team to stand up and take the audience's warm applause and then entertained them with a string of jokes that included a few gently aimed at the opponents, Leeds United. 'The Leeds manager, Don Revie, he's had them doing special training for the FA Cup Final. He placed 11 dustbins on the pitch, and he told his players to weave in and out of them as part of their training. I think you are going to be all right boys, the dustbins won 2-1.'

On the day of the big game, Liverpool's trip from their Weybridge hotel proved anything but easy – en route, the hired police motorcyclist failed to show up, and the team looked snookered as the traffic got thicker and thicker the nearer the coach got to Wembley. Thankfully, one of the players spotted another police motorcyclist, who was persuaded to help escort the team's coach past the vast crowds heading towards the stadium.

En route, Shankly ordered the coach driver to turn up the volume on the radio. Why? It was because Shankly himself was the 'castaway' on that week's edition of that long-running BBC Radio show *Desert Island Discs*. The players were doubled up with laughter as the manager's taste of music invaded the nation. Scottish songs and singers mainly, Kenneth McKellar's 'A Red, Red Rose' among them, and finally, of course, Gerry and the Pacemakers with 'You'll Never Walk Alone'.

Shankly's choice of book to accompany the programme's staple literary fare of the Bible and the complete works of William Shakespeare was a compilation of stories by the Scottish writer, John Buchan (who wrote the famous thriller, *The 39 Steps*). Shankly didn't miss the opportunity to tell the legendary presenter, Roy Plomley: 'There are also 39 steps leading up to the Royal Box at Wembley. And my boys will be ascending them to receive the FA Cup.'

He chose 'Liverpool Football Club' as his luxury item, so 'I can continue my work creating a great football club.' Single-minded. What, Bill Shankly?!

As the Liverpool players readied themselves in the dressing room, comedian Jimmy Tarbuck and well-loved singer Frankie Vaughan briefly dropped in to wish good luck to Shankly's men – the Leeds United dressing room was locked to outsiders. It was time to get down to business.

***

If the great bard, William Shakespeare, could pen a series of stunning soliloquies for leading characters in his thought-provoking and sumptuous plays, how about this address from Bill Shankly. Minutes ahead of his team's contest against Don Revie's Leeds United, who had just been pipped to winning the league championship on goal average in the very week leading up to the final, and a side expected to give the Scotsman's red-shirted warriors the toughest of tough battles:

> Leeds are honoured and lucky to be on the same pitch as you. You will win because you are fitter, harder and more skilled. You will win because you must not disappoint the finest supporters in the world.
>
> Enjoy yourselves out there, boys, be professional, do all your running and tackling, but don't forget to enjoy it all, every minute of it, and that way you will always remember what happens today. It will be one of your best memories. This is a great day in our lives.

***

It was raining heavily as Prince Philip went out on to the Wembley pitch to meet the teams before the kick-off; the reigning monarch, Queen Elizabeth II, was already seated in the Royal Box – and delighted the huge Liverpool following by being dressed in red.

'Ee-Aye-Addio, the Queen is dressed in Red,' thundered down from the massed Liverpool support. The official ticket allocation had been a much-criticised 15,000 for each club, but the noise around the stadium suggested the Liverpool support was of a greater number than that. One of the great anomalies of the old Wembley Stadium – capacity 100,000 – was that the management and coaching personnel of both clubs would sit literally side by side on a long wooden bench open to whatever the inclement weather conditions could occur on any day.

On 1 May 1965, it poured down – and there are great pictures of Liverpool's Bob Paisley, Reuben Bennett, the injured Gordon Milne, and Bill Shankly, heads protected from the rain with macs and tracksuit tops, sitting right alongside Leeds United's Syd Owen, Don Revie and Les Cocker, also well wrapped up, with only a quiet young ball boy sat between them. A photograph of its time.

The match had barely started before a frightening and foul tackle by the Leeds United's captain, Bobby Collins, heavily felled Liverpool full-back Gerry Byrne. While trainer Bob Paisley, treated his knee, Byrne made light of the real injury that the Collins tackle had caused him. He had, in fact, sustained a broken collarbone. Despite being in extreme pain, the heroic full-back played out the rest of the game – with the Leeds players unaware of Byrne's major problem.

It was lauded at the time, and still to this day it is recognised as one of the greatest displays of bravery by any player in Liverpool' s illustrious history. The game itself was something of a bore, Liverpool the dominant force, Leeds seemingly a little overawed by the occasion. Goalless after 90 minutes. To adapt a line from the great bard himself: it was a clear case of Much Ado About Nothing ... Nothing!

Liverpool eventually went ahead three minutes into extra time when Gerry Byrne played his part as Roger Hunt stooped to head a cross into the net. The stalemate was broken. The noise in the Liverpool crowd was off the scale, but Leeds reacted positively to going behind by rustling up an equaliser through Billy Bremner.

The game was settled in the 111th minute of the contest, when a cross from Ian Callaghan, who had been an injury scare throughout the build-up to the final, was met brilliantly with a diving header from Scottish centre-forward Ian St John:

> The sweetest moment of my football life. Willie Stevenson worked Ian Callaghan away on the right and Cally, as always, timed his cross perfectly. For some reason, Gary Sprake, the Leeds' keeper, came off his line to get the ball, against all the odds, and I went past him to meet it. The Leeds line was guarded by their right-back, Paul Reaney. but the net seemed huge to me now, and I headed the ball with a heavy bump. It flew home!

Liverpool had won the FA Cup … finally. Ron Yeats and his team-mates walked up those famous 39 steps and received the FA Cup from a smiling Queen, resplendent in red. The next few minutes at Wembley was a blur of celebration, great relief and sheer exhilaration – around the pitch as the Liverpool players did a riotous lap of honour, and on the terraces and in the stands as the Liverpool fans made it very clear that after a wait that stretched back decades … 'All's Well That Ends Well'.

Back in Liverpool there were mass celebrations, and when the team returned home the following day they were welcomed by a huge crowd estimated at around 250,000. I was one of those 250,000 … just. My dad, a police officer, was on crowd-control duty that afternoon, which was difficult in itself, as hundreds of people were hurt in crushes as they waited patiently for the team to arrive back at Lime

Street Station from London and parade in an open-topped bus around the city centre.

My brother David and I were driven down to the homecoming by our mum, who had just passed her driving test. It was her *first* solo drive, so the journey to and from the city centre on incredibly busy roads full of impatient motorists and a deadline to make was as memorable as standing five deep and only five feet tall trying to get a glimpse of our returning heroes and that famous trophy.

We *did* see the coach, the players and the trophy as it made its journey towards the city's town hall but it was all over in a flash. My brother and I saw very little, had to contend with having our mum having driving hysterics, and witnessed the first embryonic signs of a later phenomenon, 'road rage', from her ungracious fellow motorists – but despite all that, we can always say we were there to see the FA Cup come home!

Added Time:

- Injured players Gordon Milne and Gerry Byrne carried the FA Cup around to a tumultuous reception at a packed Anfield ahead of the Reds' meeting with Inter Milan in the first leg of their European Cup semi-final. They won 3-1 on a very special night before going out after losing 3-0 in a controversial return leg.
- Liverpool full-back Chris Lawler was married on the Monday immediately after the FA Cup Final – and played for the Reds the following evening(!) against Inter Milan.
- Both Roger Hunt and Ian St John scored headed goals in the cup final. Hunt had scored a headed goal at Wembley before, on his England debut against Austria in April 1962, and Ian St John had actually

scored a header for Scotland against England at the stadium just a few weeks before the final.

- Geoff Strong graciously offered his cup final shirt to the man he had replaced in the match, Gordon Milne. Milne thanked Strong for such a kind gesture but declined the offer. Milne was later to receive a winner's medal.
- As is customary at the presentation of the FA Cup, the goalkeeper would be behind the winning captain and carry the base. In Peter Kenny Jones's biography of Tommy Lawrence, he tells the story that a little later Bill Shankly asked his keeper where the base was – '"I've no idea, boss, I didn't even know I had it." I'd lost the bloody FA Cup plinth. I felt awful. At the post-match function later that evening the boss shouted over, "We've found it!" "Where was it, boss?" I said nervously. "I'll tell you where it was, in Southend, in a coach, on the top shelf. And that's about as far away as you were to Billy Bremner's volley in the final this afternoon."'
- The Liverpool players were each paid a £1,000 bonus and Tommy Smith spent some of it on his first car – a Morris 1100. And he loved it.
- Liverpool's classy wing-half Willie Stevenson summed up the whole experience of winning the FA Cup Final perfectly: 'It was simply the best time of our lives.'

Chapter 3

1970s: Just the Ticket … Again and Again!

1971

The bar had been set very high for the new decade – the 60s had been an absolute blast for many people and had gone out with the ultimate stellar moment when man walked on the Moon for the first time. It was a simply epic moment – the ultimate journey into the unknown conquered.

'That's one small step for man. One giant leap for mankind.' American astronaut Neil Armstrong's famous words as he and his fellow astral pioneer, Buzz Aldrin, descended from their lunar capsule to walk on the Moon's surface on 20 July 1969 were unforgettable. Unbelievably, we all watched it happen live on the small black-and-white TV sets in the corner of our living rooms with pictures sent directly from the Moon itself. Amazing. It sent out the 60s on a triumphant note.

Back on planet Earth, the new decade, the 1970s, and the new year, 1970 itself, got the ball rolling – and two of that year's cultural events are noteworthy. Firstly, after nearly ten years of setting the world alight with their remarkable music, The Beatles broke up – and each of the Fab Four went their own way.

Meanwhile, in September 1970, a musical event, the Worthy Farm Pop, Blues and Folk Festival, took place, almost unnoticed, with about 1,500 people in attendance. We would know it now as Glastonbury – simply the biggest music festival in the world, with the biggest bands and most famous rock stars queueing up to be invited to play on its famous stages – and 300,000 fans queueing up to get into the three-day rock extravaganza, rain or more rain, mud or more mud!

The two most watched TV shows in the UK in 1970 were *Miss World* and *The Benny Hill Show*, which tells its own story, in a year when the first national Women's Liberation Conference was held.

In sport, England lost to West Germany in the World Cup quarter-finals in Mexico – their four-year reign as world champions was over. It was the World Cup where all football enthusiasts fell back in love with a Brazilian side graced with players such as the incomparable Pelé, captain Carlos Alberto, red-hot striker Jairzinho and free-kick supremo Rivelino. The tournament fell right over the weeks I was taking my O level exams – which duly suffered considerably as a result!

And on Merseyside, Everton, with that brilliant midfield trio of Harvey, Ball and Kendall, had been deservedly crowned league champions.

Meanwhile, over at Stanley Park, times were about to change, with 21 February 1970 becoming a very significant date. A shock 1-0 defeat for Liverpool at Second Division Watford in their FA Cup quarter-final all but brought the curtain down on Bill Shankly's 'first' great team. Record goalscorer Roger Hunt had already left the club to join Bolton Wanderers in December 1969, and Barry Endean's headed winner for Watford on a ploughed field of a pitch led the Anfield careers of stalwarts Tommy Lawrence, Ron Yeats and Ian St John to be drawn to a close. The average age of the side Liverpool fielded at Vicarage Road was 27 years.

Fifteen months later, Bill Shankly would proudly lead out his 'new' team at Wembley Stadium for the FA Cup Final, on 8 May 1971, average age 24 years, three months. Players such as goalkeeper Ray Clemence, full-back Alec Lindsay, centre-half Larry Lloyd, wingmen and fellow university graduates Brian Hall and Steve Heighway and £100,000 signing from Cardiff John Toshack were being moulded into a formidable team that was an exciting mix of youth and experience.

And 1965 FA Cup winners such as Chris Lawler, Ian Callaghan and new captain Tommy Smith along with established team-mates Emlyn Hughes and Alun Evans would make up the Reds starting line-up in the 1971 FA Cup Final against Arsenal – and Peter Thompson would make a significant contribution as substitute when the 1965 FA Cup winner entered the fray.

The Reds' journey to Wembley had seen them narrowly beat Aldershot in the third round, who had player-manager, former Red, Jimmy Melia in their line-up. In the fourth round Swansea were put to the sword, 3-0 at Anfield. Chris Lawler popped up with the winner, as he often did, in their fifth-round Anfield tie with Southampton. A tough twin set of games against fancied Tottenham Hotspur was won by a single goal scored by Steve Heighway in a replay at White Hart Lane, following a goalless draw at Anfield.

The FA Cup semi-final paired the Merseyside giants Everton and Liverpool together in a derby match played in front of a packed crowd at Old Trafford. Alan Ball put Everton ahead in the first half but the Reds rallied in the second half with super goals from Alun Evans and Brian Hall to book Liverpool a trip to Wembley. The club's third visit to the Twin Towers.

Leaving Old Trafford that afternoon, my dad and I heard fellow spectators saying Stoke City were beating favourites Arsenal in the other semi-final. We were all pleased with that news because the team from the Potteries represented a potentially easier opponent in the Wembley showpiece than the in-form Arsenal. However, as we piled into Dad's old Morris Minor, the radio gave out the news that Arsenal had scrambled a late equaliser – and they subsequently went on to win the replay.

By the time the FA Cup Final came around, Arsenal had already won the first leg of the double, clinching the league title at White Hart Lane of all places. Arsenal had beaten Liverpool in the 1950 FA Cup Final, and they were favourites to repeat that feat against Shankly's 'new' team that had finished a creditable fifth at the end of the league season. It was the classic north vs south encounter that worked so well for TV and the news media – and the match got a huge build-up as the big day approached. Bryan Cowgill, the then much respected BBC Head of Sport, said, 'I've always believed that north-south battles in English football produce the best skills and the widest entertainment.'

The two league fixtures between the clubs had both finished 2-0 for the home teams – John Toshack and Tommy Smith, with a penalty, securing the points for Liverpool at Anfield. It was all to play for. And in the week of the FA Cup Final, among the excitement and anticipation of the big match to come, Liverpool quietly made the signing of a young player from Scunthorpe United – his name: Kevin Keegan. Going forward, he would be Shankly's final piece in the jigsaw.

* * *

The late Peter Robinson was a hugely influential figure in Liverpool Football Club's massive upward trajectory in the 35 years of service he gave the club. PBR, as he was known around the corridors, joined the club in 1965 as secretary, and would finish his time at Anfield as Chief Executive and a board member. His commitment to the task of building the club's reputation, influence and on-field success was immense. He had an important relationship with the long-serving chairman, Sir John Smith, and all the managers who passed through Anfield during his time at the club, and with the various governing bodies here and abroad. He was also an important figure in the aftermath of Heysel and Hillsborough. His manner was understated, pragmatic, diplomatic and personable – and he managed his busy working life very well.

I had lots of business meetings with him down the years – and we occasionally shared a bottle of his favourite red wine, Barolo, and he would talk about his other great love, cricket, as well as all things Anfield.

In the build-up to the 1971 FA Cup Final, Peter Robinson reflected on the range of tasks and responsibilities that befell him and his team, increased from five colleagues to eight, in the six weeks' build-up to the big Wembley occasion:

> Just what is entailed between the semi-final and the moment the FA Cup is finally won? It involves six weeks of working about 80 to 90 hours flat out. People don't generally realise but we are not planning for one final but two. Every detail for a cup final replay has to be planned too.
>
> The problems fall into seven main categories: 1. the fans, 2. the team, 3. the directors and officials, 4. the banquet, 5. the return, 6. the possible replay, 7. public relations. The fans, of course, means tickets. You can't get a quart into a pint pot, no more than 46,000, our average gate, can share 20,000 tickets. No matter which way you allocate the tickets, we can't please everybody, but we like to think we have been fair. We have had very few

complaints about our ticket arrangements for this year's FA Cup Final.

The time-consuming part of the operation is dealing with most of the operation through the post. This alone means opening about 30,000 envelopes and replying to everyone. Although we ask fans not to apply for tickets unless they qualify, we get literally thousands of heart-rending appeals. We had one letter opened this morning from a man in prison who is a red-hot Liverpudlian and is due to be released in the week of the final!

We have booked a hotel in North London for the players, ten twin rooms and a dozen single rooms, and arranged with one of London's leading amateur clubs to use their pitch for training on Friday morning – and have also reserved a section of the Palladium for the team on the Friday night. We have sent more than 300 invitations out for the post-match banquet for club personnel, including the directors, players, staff and their wives. Press and TV representatives, some of the club's largest shareholders, representatives from the clubs Liverpool beat on the way to Wembley, representatives from Lancashire, and all neighbouring clubs.

Guests from the FA, the Football League, the Central League, the Lancashire League – in all of whose competitions Liverpool compete – civic dignitaries, the Scottish, Welsh and Irish FAs, Stanley Rous, Chairman of the Fairs Cup Committee, and Hans Bangerter, Secretary of UEFA. Then, of course, there is the return home to Liverpool of around 100 people to be planned for the following day. We will follow what Everton

> did in 1968 and get off the train on the outskirts of the city and in a cavalcade of coaches make a tour of the city before a reception at St George's Hall.
>
> Of course, if the match at Wembley is a draw, I and my staff will have to be back early because we shall be selling replay tickets on the Sunday. We must cater for a replay [the previous year's FA Cup Final between Leeds United and Chelsea had indeed gone to a replay, held on the following Thursday evening at Old Trafford]. Liverpool get many press and TV inquiries during the normal course of a season but at cup final time this doubles, and even trebles, and has to be dealt with.

An insight into the scale of preparations to be dealt with both ahead of, and after, the big afternoon at Wembley. And, after all that, a nice quiet day at a cricket match for Peter Robinson with a large glass of Bolero in his hand would seem to have been very well deserved!!

***

An FA Cup Final Ticket

For many decades, the hunt for the elusive strip of cardboard that gave you access to the big day at Wembley and a lifetime's memories was the stuff of legend ... and myth. We are into 'Holy Grail' territory.

As a fan, the search started the moment the final whistle went at the semi-final and your team was in the biggest domestic game of the year – indeed, an international event. Everybody knew somebody who didn't deserve a ticket but had got one. Everybody knew somebody who said they had a 'spare' but it never materialised. Everybody knew somebody who would travel down on spec, and everybody knew somebody who was prepared to swap or sell theirs. Some fans would sell their car to get a ticket for the final, while others would sell their ticket to get the car!

A match between two sides that could attract a crowd around 40,000 if it were a mid-season league game could comfortably attract three or four times that if billed as the FA Cup Final. And in 1971 I was introduced to the dilemma … how do I get a cup final ticket? A touch ironic, given the future path my career path took!

But in 1971 my search was genuine – and the chances genuinely remote. I was a regular attendee at home games at Anfield but wasn't a season ticket holder. I didn't have any influential friends in either high (or low) places and I didn't have any significant money – only my weekly pocket money, which would just about cover the cost of the cup final programme. At 16, still at school, and not used to travelling long distances on my own, the whole thing looked a hopeless case, and I had reluctantly settled for a Saturday afternoon in front of the TV watching the match … but I made it to Wembley Stadium on the big day, and this is how.

I had been to Wembley Stadium the year before on a school trip to watch England vs Northern Ireland – it was a night match, and England's final home game before starting their defence of being world champions in Mexico. I still remember walking into the stadium and just being blown away by the sheer size of the arena – and under the floodlights with the famous Wembley pitch it all looked magical, just a very special place. A year on, and my previous trip to Wembley coupled with my love affair with the Reds meant I lived in hope that something might come up for me.

And it did! I got a ticket for the 1971 FA Cup Final via a lucky number on the end of a coupon given out at a Liverpool match against Newcastle United at Anfield a few weeks before the final. If the coupon you were given as you entered Anfield ended in 1, you had the right to buy a ticket. I say 'lucky'; in fact, it was my brother, David, who got the coupon as I was on another school trip, this time to the Netherlands to play football, and missed the game at Anfield.

The first question I asked my parents as they picked me up from Speke Airport at the end of our Dutch adventure was: 'Any luck with getting me a ticket for the FA Cup Final?' Their silence was deafening, and I knew something was up. Then the news of the 'magic voucher' was broken to me. It was the moment to fight my corner, fairly or unfairly.

I put forward my case for the much-sought-after ticket. Fan for ten years, lived and breathed the club, scrapbooks, programmes, autographs, never missed a home game (except one!). Trips to Melwood in school holidays to watch the team train. Properly brought up into the Anfield experience by going to plenty of reserve games before I was allowed to watch the 'big heads' (as Ronnie Moran called the first team). It was all there in red and white.

High-level diplomacy, well, furious family rows, took place in the days building up to the final on 'who deserved the precious ticket most', before I secured the prize – and on Saturday, 8 May I set off on a football special from Lime Street to Wembley. To be honest, travelling on my own to the final – discounting the other 20,000 fans – was a little daunting, but with my precious ticket stuffed strategically down the front of my trousers for safekeeping, off I went. I was back at Wembley ... and so were Liverpool.

* * *

Peter Robinson's planning was going along perfectly – as we had come to expect from the highly respected sports executive. The only thing PBR couldn't stage-manage was the weather, although I'm sure he would have tried. In 1950, Liverpool had lost to Arsenal at Wembley in the pouring rain; in 1965, Liverpool beat Leeds United at Wembley in the pouring rain.

On 8 May 1971 the country woke up to a beautiful late spring day – in fact, by early afternoon, and in and around London, it was boiling hot. The temperature on the Wembley pitch proved exhausting for the players – and the first 90 minutes of the game was something of a goalless bore. But along with thousands of fellow Reds fans, we were still singing our hearts out behind the goal at the Tunnel End of the famous stadium.

The match came to life inside the first two minutes of extra time. Peter Thompson, on as a substitute for Alun Evans, sprinted down the left and fed Steve Heighway, who galloped down the wing before dispatching a shot that caught the Arsenal goalkeeper, Bob Wilson, napping as it went into the net at the near post. Heighway had scored a similar goal in the derby match against Everton earlier in the season. Neither goal was a fluke.

I worked for many years with Bob Wilson, not least when he was the presenter of BBC's *Football Focus* and I was the programme's producer. I would regularly tease him about the 'near-post' goal at Wembley – and he would pull me up short by reminding me of the match's final score.

After the goal went in, we all went mad. Then in the middle of a raucous rendition of 'We love you, Liverpool, we do … we love you, Liverpool, we do … we love you Liverpool …', the singing stopped … *instantly*. Arsenal had equalised.

Whether it was George Graham or substitute Eddie Kelly who was officially credited with the goal, it was a scrappy effort – and the Liverpool defenders rued its scoring. Liverpool captain Tommy Smith: 'It was one of the softest goals Wembley had ever witnessed.'

Eight minutes from time, and with a replay that Peter Robinson had had to plan for looking a distinct possibility,

Charlie George scored the decisive goal. Some 25 yards out, the young Arsenal forward hit a speculative shot that took a deflection off Larry Lloyd and sped past Ray Clemence. Arsenal had won the double ... and Shankly's men cursed their luck. The Liverpool boss had his own take on proceedings. He felt that Liverpool's shirts became heavy with perspiration in the blazing sunshine and were like 'sacks on the backs' of his players.

The return home to Liverpool on the following day was a remarkable occasion and, once again, hundreds of thousands of Liverpool fans turned out in a show of support for their Anfield favourites. And, in a special thank you to the crowds, Shankly delivered one of his most famous speeches. This time, outside St George's Hall in the city centre: 'Ladies and gentlemen, yesterday at Wembley, we may have lost the cup, but you, the people, have won everything. You have won over the policemen in London. You won over the London public, and it is questionable if Chairman Mao's China could have arranged such a show of strength as you have shown yesterday and today.'

The multitudes roared their approval. And I was delighted to be one of them.

1974

In the summer of 1974, there were two seismic resignations that shook the world. On Friday, 9 August, Richard Nixon resigned as the President of the United States of America, the first American to essentially be removed from the Oval Office following his involvement in the famous Watergate scandal. He left the White House by helicopter – a chastened man. Big, big news.

Four weeks earlier, Bill Shankly, the true founder of the modern Liverpool Football Club, resigned as its manager. In some parts of the world, bigger news!

Both men were born in 1913, both men were huge public figures, but I know which one caused the biggest shock waves in my and many other people's lives. Politics is important, but football – on Merseyside – is a religion, and having one of its legendary leaders stepping down from a role he had made his own was both sudden and totally unexpected.

Some years later, Shankly, in typically colourful prose, described it as 'the most difficult thing in the world, when I went to tell the chairman. It was like walking to the electric chair. That's the way I felt.'

Peter Robinson reflected, 'The Board were desperate for him to stay in any capacity. He could have any job he wanted. He said he was tired and needed a rest, so we said he could come in once a week, if he wanted. But Bill was adamant and if I couldn't persuade him, no one else could.'

On Saturday, 10 August 1974, Richard Nixon settled back into an armchair in his home, La Casa, on San Clemente, California, ready to contemplate a whole new life. Meanwhile, 5,000 miles away in London, Bill Shankly was leading out his beloved Reds at Wembley for the final time. It was a kind gesture by the club, as Liverpool were at the Twin Towers to play Leeds United in that year's FA Charity Shield. The Reds had just won the FA Cup at Wembley four months before, and if you ventured a thought then that the charismatic Scotsman wouldn't be the manager for the following season, people would have thought that you were mad.

That FA Charity Shield made headlines of its own, which we will return to in due course, but Shankly and his loyal group of players had enjoyed another special Wembley moment back in May – and in some style.

* * *

Following the defeat in the 1971 FA Cup Final, Shankly continued to bed in his 'new' team and central to that was the human dynamo that was Kevin Keegan. He was the young Doncaster lad who Liverpool had bought in that cup final week. He joined his new team-mates at Wembley, and, to help him settle in, he and his girlfriend, Jean, were both invited to the post-match banquet.

I saw his debut for Liverpool in a pre-season match against Tranmere Rovers at Prenton Park a few months later. While the first-team squad was over in Germany playing a batch of friendlies, Ronnie Moran took charge of the players left behind, including Keegan. His performance against Tranmere Rovers, where he had starred on the Wirral in the previous season's FA Cup competition for Scunthorpe United, didn't impress Moran, who thought he hadn't stuck to instructions, but all the people I joined on the ferry back to Liverpool were only talking about one young man – Kevin Keegan.

A four-goal haul in the annual pre-season Reds vs Whites match encouraged Shankly to put non-stop, no-fear Keegan straight into the first team for their opening league match of the 1971/72 season against Nottingham Forest at Anfield. As luck would have it, BBC's *Match of the Day* cameras were at the game and captured Kevin Keegan scoring in the 12th minute. It was a scrappy sort of goal, but the nation had been introduced to the talented lad from Doncaster.

He started 35 league games that season, scoring nine goals. The following campaign he played 41 league games, scoring 13 goals in a title-winning team, and a further four goals in the Reds' successful UEFA Cup success. League champions and European trophy winners, Liverpool were back where they belonged and Kevin Keegan was en route to becoming a Kop favourite.

* * *

Phil Thompson, the young Liverpool defender who had forced his way into the Reds' defence towards the end of the club's tumultuous climax to the 1972/73 season with league championship and UEFA Cup medals, to go alongside his reserve-team title memento, was busy.

Thompson was just a few days away from playing in the FA Cup Final at Wembley. But first there was a job to do nearer to home. He was helping his Liverpool-mad mum make two big banners with 'Shanks Red Army' on one and 'LFC – SUPER REDS' on the other. They would unfurl at Wembley on the big day.

He had watched the iconic 1965 FA Cup Final on TV, before going to Anfield with his mum and brother, Owen, to watch Liverpool, on a famous night, dismantle the reigning European and world champions, Inter Milan, three days later. Thompson attended the 1971 FA Cup Final, at the time 'one of the worst moments of my life, although it was a great thrill for me just to go to Wembley'.

A Scouser through and through, Thompson's pipe-cleaner build defied logic in the manner he could physically match his broader-beamed opponents, such as Newcastle United's Malcolm Macdonald. He was a clever young player, with a football brain ahead of his years, who put every last inch of his heart and soul into every match he played for Liverpool – all 477 of them.

Another player who would be appearing in the FA Cup Final was Scotsman Peter Cormack – a shrewd Shankly signing, a clever midfield man who seemed to play on his tiptoes but was a pivotal part of Liverpool's success in their 1972/73 season of dual success, in domestic and European competitions. Cormack, who sadly passed away in 2024, had relished the thought of playing in his first FA Cup Final: 'Playing in the FA Cup Final at Wembley was unquestionably top of the to-do list for every professional footballer.'

The third player making his FA Cup Final debut was Kevin Keegan, whose impact on Shankly's 'new' team was simply profound. The Reds' route to Wembley had started with a home third-round tie against bottom of the Fourth Division Doncaster Rovers at Anfield. And a bit like their 1965 tie against Stockport County, the big 'upset' was on when, after Doncaster-born Keegan had given the Reds an early lead, the South Yorkshire side equalised and then went ahead and stayed ahead for a good 40 minutes.

It was Keegan again who pulled the Reds level, and they survived a late scare when Rovers hit the bar. A replay win in Yorkshire was followed by another replay success against Carlisle, then a comfortable fifth-round win over Ipswich Town. A tough 1-0 victory at Bristol City in the quarter-final led to a replay win over Leicester City in the semi-final, including a wonderful Keegan goal, which all got the Reds to Wembley to face Joe Harvey's Newcastle United.

Kevin Keegan scored twice in the final, and Heighway added another goal to his cup final tally ... 3-0, as comprehensive a win in an FA Cup Final for many years. Newcastle were simply outclassed, their big star and 'big noise' Malcolm Macdonald, with his pre-match boasts, completely boxed off by Phil Thompson. 'Super Mac is only good when it's raining,' we all sang – and nothing came back.

Keegan's second goal, Liverpool's third, was masterful – an 11-pass move began with the intention of keeping the ball, but Tommy Smith played a clever one-two with Steve Heighway, and then pulled the ball back to an unmarked Kevin Keegan, who side-footed it home.

Emlyn Hughes, now the Reds skipper, lifted the trophy – job done. As the Anfield heroes did their lap of honour, Bill Shankly walked quietly to the dressing room, but not before two adoring fans ran on to the playing area and bent down in front of the proud Scotsman. 'While you are down there, would you mind giving my shoes a quick polish,' joked Shankly.

For two Kirkby boys, contrasting emotions. Thompson exchanged his shirt with Newcastle's Terry McDermott. The two would later become Liverpool team-mates, as would the Newcastle full-back Alan Kennedy, who would make his own very important mark in Liverpool's history.

The Liverpool team got an incredulous reception of around 500,000 people on their return to the city the following day. As always, the massive crowd came to a complete hush to hear Bill Shankly's wise words:

> I think today I feel prouder than I have ever done before. I said three years ago we would go back to Wembley. Not only did the team win the cup yesterday, they gave an exhibition of football. But above all, we are pleased for you. It's you we play for. It's you who pay our wages. Not only did we win the cup on the field, but we won it on the terraces as well.

It was a special time to be a Liverpudlian, the team in full bloom, the supporters in full voice and then, just weeks later, the great Bill Shankly called it full time on his illustrious Anfield career. Remarkable.

Although Bob Paisley had assumed the role of Liverpool's manager, the club decided that the retiring Bill Shankly should enjoy one last hurrah – and the 1974 FA Charity Shield provided that opportunity. The season's opener had moved to Wembley to reinvigorate its importance – indeed, Liverpool had played in the 1971 match as losing finalists in the FA Cup against Leicester City, who had just won promotion from the Second Division. The Foxes won the game at Filbert Street 1-0. Arsenal, the double winners, were on an overseas tour.

On 10 August 1974, Shankly proudly led his team out for the last time, with the new Leeds United manager, Brian

Clough, clapping gently alongside him. That was the last of the 'Sweet Charity', as the match was between two teams who couldn't resist a challenge.

The game's high spot, or rather low spot, was when FA Cup hero Kevin Keegan became an FA Charity Shield 'villain', throwing a punch at Leeds United skipper Billy Bremner, who responded in a similar fashion. It was totally unbecoming in a fixture of that nature. Both players were sent off – and both players compounded the incident by ripping their shirts off as they walked along the perimeter of the pitch on the way to the tunnel and their respective dressing rooms. The two players had thrown the punches, but an outraged FA reciprocated by 'throwing the book' at them – and both served long suspensions.

The match itself ended 1-1 – and the 1973/74 Player of the Year, Ian Callaghan, stepped up to score the vital winning spot kick in the subsequent penalty shoot-out. Shankly left Wembley a happy man, Clough left Wembley with a 'dis-united' Leeds team – and his time at Elland Road eventually lasted just 44 days.

1977

Despite his natural reticence to follow a legend like Bill Shankly into the manager's job at Anfield, Bob Paisley, who had joined the club on the brink of the Second World War, found his feet quickly. No great orator, his team talks spun out in his native North East accent were not always fully understood by his players but, in time, they got the message. Bob really knew his stuff – and Bob was not to be messed around with.

For a short while, there was a little awkwardness as Shankly, still settling into his new life, would turn up on a regular basis at Melwood, which confused the players. Who did they address and as what? Diplomatically, it was sorted out; Shankly was asked not to attend training and suchlike, and Bob was left to his own devices.

The Reds finished runners-up to Derby County in Paisley's first season in charge, and in his second season as boss, the horse-racing lover finally went clear, as Liverpool won the title from QPR in their final match of the season against Wolves at Molineux.

The league title done and dusted, Paisley's men were crowned UEFA Cup winners in a tight two-legged final against a talented Club Brugge side. They were destined to meet again two years later for an even bigger prize – and at an iconic venue.

The year of 1977 was when 'The King', Elvis Presley, died, and, in London, glam rock star Marc Bolan was killed in a car crash. The first Brits Awards were held and a new wave of music was with us – punk rock, led by, among others, the Sex Pistols, who managed to offend and entertain in equal measure. They were tabloid heaven.

The nation celebrated Queen Elizabeth II's Silver Jubilee, the first London to New York Concorde flights took off and one of cinema's most well-loved sequence of films was released – *Star Wars*.

In sport, Virginia Wade won the Ladies Singles at Wimbledon, and, at Aintree, history was made when Red Rum, ridden by Tommy Stack, won a third Grand National. Red Rum is recognised as the horse who 'saved the National', which was beginning to lose its lustre. He was the people's champion, winning the famous race in 1973, 1974 and then, almost impossibly, in 1977.

Bob Paisley's Liverpool side were fast becoming football thoroughbreds – winning the league championship for a second year running, and by reaching the European Cup Final, not least by conquering the talented French side, Saint-Étienne in an absorbing last-eight second leg at Anfield.

In the FA Cup, the Reds had also marched to the final via wins against Crystal Palace, Carlisle United, Oldham Athletic and Middlesbrough. In the semi-final, they had an epic encounter against neighbours Everton, at Maine Road. The first match ended 2-2, with the Toffees claiming, with some justification, that a late 'winning goal' by Bryan Hamilton had been wrongly rubbed out by controversial Welsh referee Clive Thomas. The anger over at Goodison Park still lingers.

Liverpool, with goals from Neal, Case and Ray Kennedy, got the job done four days later at Maine Road. They would meet Manchester United in the FA Cup Final at Wembley, just four days before playing in their first European Cup Final in Rome against Borussia Mönchengladbach.

A remarkable treble was up for grabs. The excitement building up for the Liverpool fans who had booked their train tickets for the unlikely journey of Lime Street to Rome, myself included, could be excused on this unprecedented occasion for looking upon the FA Cup Final as something that was more of a very tasty starter than a full-blown main course. Of course, we all wanted to win, and with it clinch the double, but the European Cup Final was all anybody was talking, and singing, about – and then circumstances played a big part in making Bob Paisley's team selection for the big Wembley occasion.

The FA had decided that any replay of the FA Cup Final wouldn't take place until 27 June – given Liverpool's date with destiny in Rome, that prevented the normal practice of any replay being staged in the week following the final. Paisley was angry with the thought of waiting 33 days for any FA Cup Final replay if needed – and his team selection for Wembley reflected that. He went for an all-out attack strategy – a 'win at all costs' plan. He opted for a three-man forward line of Keegan, Heighway and David Johnson, leaving Ian Callaghan out of the starting line-up as substitute. Paisley later admitted it was his 'worst-ever tactical decision'.

On a hot sunny day, the first half of the 1977 FA Cup Final was a bit of a bore, but three goals in the space of five early second-half minutes decided the contest. Stuart Pearson put United ahead, Jimmy Case scored a wonderful equaliser, only for a fluke of a goal in which a shot from Lou Macari found itself in the Liverpool net via deflections off Emlyn Hughes and Jimmy Greenhoff. It wasn't a goal worthy of deciding the outcome of an FA Cup Final – but it did just that.

Manchester United held on to to win – and the Liverpool squad, manager, families, directors and other members of the official party boarded the 7.45pm club-chartered train back to Lime Street that same evening. As fate would have it, one of the football specials ahead of the club's train had broken down, and what would normally have been a real 'pain' turned into something very different.

Bob Paisley: 'It turned into a positive thing for us – the delay gave the players a chance to let their hair down and by the time we got off at Lime Street they had well and truly got Wembley out of their system.'

They were up for it. And so was I!

1978

Liverpool's glorious victory in Rome over the German champions, Borussia Mönchengladbach, was a crowning moment for the club. It was a very special night – and memories of it still resound to this day. It was a night when everything came together. Veni, vini, vici.

Goals from Terry McDermott, a brilliant headed goal from Tommy Smith (!) and a neatly taken penalty from Phil Neal clinched a deserved 3-1 win. And, on the night, Kevin Keegan ran the German defence, and Berti Vogts in particular, ragged. It would be a lasting memory of a player who had been the 'final piece in the jigsaw', helping Bill Shankly create a powerful 'second' team and, for Bob Paisley, to build on it by establishing a winning machine. Keegan made 323 appearances and scored 100 goals. And now he was gone. Ironically, to Germany, to play for Hamburg.

In the summer of 1977, Liverpool went out and spent a record British transfer fee at the time of £440, 000 to bring a man to the club who would excel in every capacity he subsequently performed for Liverpool Football Club – Sir Kenny Dalglish, the club's greatest player, successful manager, board director, ambassador – and a very special human being for the remarkable kindness, dedication and duty he showed over many years following the Hillsborough disaster.

When he was brought to Anfield, many thought he was purchased as a direct replacement for the outgoing Keegan. It was a natural assumption – but a wrong one. 'The boss underlined to me that he didn't look to me to take over Kevin's role. He didn't want me to alter my style to be another Kevin. The only similarity was that I took over the number seven shirt. The fans welcomed me in my first game, the Charity Shield match against Manchester United at Wembley Stadium. We drew 0-0 and the crowd were good to me.'

He would be back at Wembley at the end of the season and make a substantial entry into the game's history books – and one of the stadium's fondest memories for legions of Reds fans. Earlier, in May 1977, Liverpool had also secured the services of another Scotsman who would also make a huge impact at Anfield over a lengthy period. Classy defender Alan Hansen was bought from Partick Thistle for £100,000.

The final £352,000 purchase of classy midfielder, Graeme Souness, from Middlesbrough in January 1978, completed the signings of a magnificent trio of Scottish soccer icons who would grace Liverpool Football Club, season in, season out, for many years to come. Their collective number of Liverpool appearances comes up just short of a remarkable 1,500 – and 241 goals, 172 of them from Kenny Dalglish.

And, in the 1978 European Cup Final against Belgian champions, Club Brugge, staged that year at Wembley Stadium, they all played their part in taking the beautiful trophy back to where it had come from – Anfield.

* * *

Liverpool only had a fleeting romance with the Football League Cup in its early days before it blossomed into a full-on 'love affair' in the early 1980s. The 'second' domestic cup competition was the brainchild of Football League Secretary Alan Hardaker, and essentially a midweek fixture programme that took advantage of the growing use of floodlights.

It started its life in the 1960/61 season, with the Reds beating Luton Town in a replay before losing to Southampton in the competition's third round. The first winners of the competition, which had been poorly supported by the fans, were Aston Villa. Liverpool's home gates for their matches against Luton Town and Southampton were 10,502 and 14,036 respectively.

Liverpool didn't take part in the League Cup again until the 1967/68 season, going out to Bolton Wanderers in the second round. And despite ruling the roost in domestic and European football, it was another ten seasons before the Reds made it to the final, by now a big Wembley occasion always played on a Saturday afternoon in mid-March, despite a full Football League fixture programme, and with no live TV coverage.

A crowd of 100,000 watched the 1978 Football League Cup Final between LFC and Brian Clough's Nottingham Forest. Forest would become league champions at the end of the season, having been promoted from the Second Division. Clough worked his magic, and his team, a blend of old and new names, which included former Liverpool centre-half Larry Lloyd and tough as teak Kenny Burns in a formidable back line, and Peter Shilton in goal, went on to win two successive European Cup finals, in 1978/79 and 1979/80.

For a few seasons, Liverpool and Forest locked horns in some major matches, Forest often coming out on top. Their 18-year-old goalkeeper, Chris Woods, was the star man for Forest at Wembley, producing save after save as the match remained goalless after 90 minutes and extra time.

The replay, played four days later at Old Trafford in front of over 54,000 fans, was won by Forest by a single goal. Phil Thompson's 54th-minute tackle on John O'Hare looked to be outside the penalty area, but experienced referee Pat Partridge gave a penalty – and John Robertson stepped up to score from the spot.

* * *

Now if I was ever asked to name my top 20 Liverpool matches from over more than 60 years of watching them, you would expect every European Cup Final win to be among them – naturally. Well, for me, the 1978 European Cup Final between Liverpool and Club Brugge would make it, but with some reservations.

Why? Firstly, because it was a fairly dull match, with Brugge, in particular, defensive and uninspiring; and secondly, because having gone through the special adventures of travelling by rail to Rome and back the previous year – an odyssey that lasted five days – a return train journey from Lime Street to Wembley seemed a little mundane by comparison.

There were incredible upsides, of course, not least that the whole of Wembley Stadium seemed to be dressed in red – 92,000 spectators in the famous old stadium and the vast majority of them being Liverpudlians. All the songs and chants were about their Anfield heroes.

The winning goal, in the 65th minute, was also a wonderful piece of football, conjured up by the Scottish duo, Graeme Souness feeding a clever pass to Kenny Dalglish, whose momentary physical and mental dexterity combined to score a bewitching chipped goal – and his celebratory leap over the advertising hoardings, a moment of sheer joy we all shared. And, once again, Liverpool skipper Emlyn Hughes lifted 'old big ears', that wonderful European Cup, a star in its own right, to the sound of a Scouse-filled Wembley Stadium going bonkers.

Terrific; then it was back to the station and all crammed on to a series of the football specials and back home. All in the space of 12 hours. Us 'Roman Veterans' felt a little short-changed. But we were European champions – again. Get over it!

Added Time:

- Liverpool played at Wembley nine times in the 1970s – a European Cup Final, three FA Cup finals, a Football League Cup Final and four FA Charity Shield matches – the last being a standout 3-1 win over Arsenal in August 1979 in the season's annual curtain-raiser.
- A disappointed Phil Boersma left Wembley Stadium before the start of the 1974 FA Cup Final when Chris Lawler was preferred as Liverpool's substitute on that day. He was back at Wembley three months later to score Liverpool's goal in their FA Charity Shield tussle with Leeds United.
- When Liverpool beat Club Brugge in the European Cup Final, Brian Clough said, 'Bob Paisley has broken this silly myth that nice guys don't win anything.'

- It became a regular occurrence to see the Scottish trio of Dalglish, Souness and Hansen have their own photograph of the 'three Jocks' lifting any trophy the Reds had just won. Tommy Smith, one of the heroes of the Reds' European Cup triumph in Rome, was on course to play in the 1978 final at Wembley too when, while working on his new house, a sledgehammer fell from a wall and landed on his foot. A broken toe was the result – and the hard man of Anfield was finally felled. There is no news on what happened to the sledgehammer!!
- In the summer of 1979, long-serving Emlyn Hughes left Anfield after making 655 appearances for the Reds. He joined Wolves, with whom he won a Football League Cup winner's medal the following season to complete his set of domestic prizes.

Chapter 4

1980s: Home from Home

Part One: 1981–83, Milking It!

1981

If Liverpool had shown little interest, or had much joy, in the Football League Cup competition since its introduction in 1960 – just one final in 14 attempts – all that was about to change at the start of the 1980s.

In an extraordinary run of success, the Reds won four League Cup finals on the trot – two via replays. Coupled with a run of four Charity Shield appearances at Wembley, it meant Liverpool had played at the national stadium an impressive eight times between 1980 and 1984, only suffering two defeats in that sequence.

Having beaten West Ham United there in thc 1980 Charity Shield 1-0 (McDermott), the two teams met again at Wembley seven months later in the 1981 Football League Cup Final. The Reds had beaten Bradford City, Swindon Town, Portsmouth, Birmingham City and Manchester City (in a two-legged semi-final) to book another capital date with the Hammers.

If the League Cup Final seemed to play second fiddle to the iconic FA Cup Final, it wasn't reflected in the crowd figure of 100,000 on 14 March 1981. 'House Full' signs would have been appropriate.

The first 90 minutes of the final were tedious, Terry McDermott having a goal ruled out for offside being a rare highlight. Liverpool's full-back Alan Kennedy was not the only player on the pitch finding the new Football League ball, with its red and blue panels, difficult to control – 'it looked out of shape and horrible' was his view. All that changed when the same Alan Kennedy, with the same 'horrible' ball, scored what seemed sure to be the winning goal with just two minutes of extra time remaining.

It was a controversial goal, not least because his shot passed over a prostrate Sammy Lee, who seemed directly in the eyeline of Hammers' goalkeeper Phil Parkes, and in an offside position. The West Ham players went crazy, but that tactic didn't always work when dealing with Welsh referee Clive Thomas, who wasn't afraid of a bit of publicity – good or bad. The goal stood.

In the dying moments of the game, Ray Clemence made a marvellous save from a Ray Stewart thunderbolt free kick. From the resultant corner Terry McDermott was forced to handle an Alvin Martin header on the goal line. Penalty! And Stewart, a deadeye Dick, from the penalty spot – he scored a remarkable 76 penalties in his West Ham career – hammered the ball wide of Clemence into the Wembley net – 1-1.

The replay, played at Villa Park 18 days later, resulted in a 2-1 win for Liverpool, Kenny Dalglish and Alan Hansen the scorers, in a match perhaps notable for just the second Reds appearance of a certain young Welsh striker, Ian Rush. He hit the woodwork in an overall impressive display that evening. As for Alan Kennedy, he would become more famous for an even more important goal that season – this time, the winning goal, in the 1981 European Cup Final against Real Madrid in Paris.

But on Wednesday, 1 April 1981, the Reds had finally proved themselves no fools again when it came to winning big matches – and Liverpool captain Phil Thompson lifted the trophy. And, another piece of silverware in the bag, Bob Paisley and his boys took the Football League Cup back to the club's trophy cabinet. More silver polish needed.

***

1982

The great Bill Shankly passed away on 29 September 1981. The dynamic creator of the modern Liverpool Football Club would be revered and respected in the many years that followed. The Red Revolution started with his appointment as Liverpool manager in 1959 and his influence still reverberates to this day.

'My idea was to build Liverpool Football Club into a bastion of invincibility. Napoleon had that idea. That's what I wanted. Liverpool would be untouchable. Up and up and up until eventually everyone would have to submit.'

I had the privilege of attending his memorial service in Liverpool Cathedral, and it was a fitting mixture of the famous and the fans. Former team-mate and Shankly's favourite player, Preston North End's Tom Finney, spoke warmly about his former colleague, as did some of his ex-players, and Ian St John gave the address. Gerry Marsden's emotional rendition of 'You'll Never Walk Alone' fittingly closed the service. At Anfield itself, the Shankly Gates and the lifelike statue erected outside the Kop are two lasting memorials to his greatness and lasting popularity of a special football man.

By this time, I was now working down in London for BBC TV Sport, with *Football Focus* and *Match of the Day* being my regular remit. The summer of 1981 marked one significant change at Anfield when, after a massive 665 appearances for Liverpool, outstanding goalkeeper Ray Clemence made a surprise move to Tottenham Hotspur.

On the day of his transfer, it was big news, and I managed to track down the 'new' Spurs keeper to a North London hotel and secured an 'exclusive' interview for that Saturday afternoon's edition of *Grandstand*.

A month later I was up at Anfield to get a *Football Focus* chat with the Reds' new goalkeeper, Bruce Grobbelaar, a colourful character with a fascinating past, which included fighting in the Bush Wars in Rhodesia and having kept goal in South Africa, Canada, USA … and Crewe Alexandra. My BBC interview with him ended with his spinning a ball on one finger, another ball on another finger, juggling with them left, right and centre around his body. It was stuff worthy of the Harlem Globetrotters.

'It was in my time in the USA I developed my repertoire of pre- and post-game gymnastics and clowning: climbing the goalposts, handstands, etc. Entertaining was ingrained into the American sporting culture.'

Over time, the Anfield Boot Room, sometimes gently and at other times firmly, persuaded him to tone down his antics – or pick the right moment to display them.

Grobbelaar made a rocky start to his Liverpool career and had contributed to a poor first half of the 1981/82 season – on Boxing Day, the Reds were unrecognisable at home against Manchester City, losing 3-1 with a miserable performance, leaving them 12th in the league, with only 24 points from 17 games. Paisley made a significant change, moving Phil Thompson aside and making Graeme Souness his new captain.

The second half of the season was a whole new ball game. The Reds' league form picked up enormously – and another Wembley date was booked. The Reds won 20 league matches after their debacle on Boxing Day – and won their 13th championship by four points, ahead of Ipswich Town – this being the first season of three points for a win, in which they ended up with 87 points.

They'd also had another cup – actually two cups – in their trophy cupboard. Why two trophies? The Football League Cup now had a title sponsor – the first of many – and Liverpool would be playing in the Football League Cup Milk Cup Final ... the Milk Cup, for short. And the winners of the 1982 final would receive the original trophy and a new one – the Milk Cup.

Liverpool's route to the 1982 final had taken a mammoth nine matches – an 11-goal two-legged savaging of Exeter City, a 4-1 win over Middlesbrough, a 3-0 replay win over Arsenal, a 3-1 replay win over Barnsley, and a 4-2 aggregate win over Ipswich Town in the competition's semi-final.

Waiting for them in the final at Wembley Stadium on 13 March were Tottenham Hotspur, managed by former Liverpool player Keith Burkinshaw.

The North London side were no strangers to the Twin Towers themselves, having won the 100th FA Cup Final there after a famous Wembley replay win against Manchester City the previous season. And they then met the league champions, Aston Villa, in a drawn FA Charity Shield match in August. They would also go on to win the 1982 FA Cup Final in a replay over Terry Venables's QPR.

Times were tough, the country was economically on its knees, a recession was biting deeply, and nowhere deeper than on Merseyside – things were tight. People were struggling and were feeling very let down by the Government. Even the city's love of football was taking a hit. Liverpool's average gate was 25 per cent down on the previous two seasons, and the playing staff would be cut in due course from 31 to 23.

Therefore, the Liverpool/Spurs Milk Cup Final clash came as something of a welcome, if brief, respite to the wider worries folk felt, and the match was watched by a capacity Wembley crowd of 100,000, raising record receipts of £720,000.

I was there with my pals, and sitting just behind us were hugely popular entertainers of the time, Russ Abbott and Les Dennis, both Reds, who were enjoying huge Saturday night TV success with *Russ Abbott's Mad House* show. Les was an old mate of mine who lived in the next street to our family home in Liverpool. We briefly exchanged thoughts on how we thought the match would go and settled down to watch it.

Ahead of the game, a lot of coverage had naturally centred around the two teams' goalkeepers, Liverpool legend Ray Clemence, now of Spurs, and Bruce Grobbelaar, his controversial Anfield replacement. Clemence: 'Obviously it is going to be special for me playing against my old team-mates. But for that first time to be a cup final at Wembley – well, it's the sort of stuff you read about in comics, fairy-tale material, and you don't think it can possibly happen. Bruce? He has had his problems being thrown in at the deep end, but confidence is never going to be one of them – if anything, he might have been over-confident and thought it was easier than he anticipated.'

Grobbelaar: 'It is the first time I have played at Wembley – and on top of that, it will be the first time I have played against Ray Clemence, and for it to be at Wembley is just brilliant.'

The 1982 final had also been built up by the media as a contest between the abrasive Reds skipper, Graeme Souness, who had begun his professional career at White Hart Lane, and the silky skills of Glenn Hoddle. It never really turned out that way. Steve Archibald put Spurs ahead in the 11th minute, Souness was heavily criticised for a tackle on Tony Galvin, unfairly in his view, and the North London side held on to the lead until the 87th minute, when one of the 'new breed' of Liverpool players, Ronnie Whelan, levelled the match at 1-1, scoring past the Reds' former great, Ray Clemence.

It was a vital goal, and a late comeback, that Russ and Les would have to catch up on later in the day because I had spotted them slipping away five minutes before the end, not expecting a late Liverpool revival.

Extra time went all Liverpool's way. Ronnie Whelan scored a second goal in the 111th minute, and Ian Rush, now becoming a fixture in the team, adding a third – the clincher – in the 119th minute. Liverpool were League Cup winners for the second year running – Milk Cup winners, the cream of the crop. And to nobody's surprise, Bruce Grobbelaar walked on his hands on the Reds' lap of honour. As you would expect!

And, the icon he had replaced at Anfield, Ray Clemence, would get a spine-tingling hero's welcome from the Kop on the final day of the 1981/82 league season. But he couldn't stop his former club clinching the title with another 3-1 win over Spurs. Mind you, he did go on to win an FA Cup winner's medal at Wembley in the replay 12 days later … but without a handstand celebration!

1983

Ahead of the 1982/83 season, Bob Paisley let it be known that it was to be his final one as the Liverpool manager, a nine-year spell of winning trophy after trophy, domestic and foreign.

The quietly spoken man, whose verbal delivery sometimes didn't match his pin-sharp knowledge of football, felt he had given the club he would have served for 44 years enough time to find his replacement – and meanwhile would go on pushing for more success. And the shy man from Hetton-le-Hole delivered on it again.

Three more trophies in his final season, as in August the Reds were back at Wembley beating Tottenham Hotspur 1-0

(Rush) in the FA Charity Shield. In March, it was back to Wembley Stadium to meet Manchester United in the 1983 Milk Cup Final – and the third victory on the trot. And in May, the Reds picked up the league championship trophy, having clinched the title as early as April.

Paisley's philosophy underpinning all this success was straightforward. He demanded that his players controlled the ball – and then pass and move. No player was allowed to stand still. 'Keep the game simple' was his mantra. Know your team-mates' strengths – and maximise the value of them. Equally, Paisley was keen that his players recognised their team-mates' weaker elements, and worked as a team to cover for them.

In the week of Bob Paisley's final home match of the 1982/83 season, BBC TV's regular midweek programme, *Sportsnight*, asked reporter Alan Parry and me to go up to Liverpool and make a film about Bob Paisley, with insights from his coaching staff, players, and family and friends – to help to reflect what made the great man tick. The opening sequence of the film remains fresh in my memory. On the day of the match, against Aston Villa, and with the league title, his sixth, already won, with the trophy to be presented that afternoon, Anfield was absolutely buzzing.

Paisley, a man who never lost his roots, unwittingly displayed that in-built humility, when he forsook all the pre-match champagne and rich buffet of meats, fish and desserts for something much simpler. As hundreds of guests enjoyed football's newly fangled corporate hospitality, we filmed a faithful old Anfield retainer carefully carrying an old wooden tray on which was placed a small bowl of vegetable soup and two Cornish pasties. On a journey the make-do waiter had no doubt made many times, he turned right at the bottom of a corridor and headed towards the door marked 'Manager'.

Inside the small, neat office was Bob Paisley, sat at his desk, dressed in his trademark cardigan, pencil in hand, working on his line-up for that afternoon's match. These were unique images – and job done, and selection decisions made, Bob settled down to his simple pre-match fare. It made a wonderful opening sequence. We felt it set the tone for the film, in which time and again people paid tribute to this seemingly 'ordinary man' with an extraordinary talent in his chosen profession.

Paisley also allowed us access to his home – and we had a lovely chat with his charming wife, Jessie. 'Life has changed all around us but we've not changed as people. I remember when Bob got £10 a week in the winter and £8 in the summer and we thought we were doing nicely then. It's all changed now, of course, but he hasn't, Bob hasn't.'

'Yes, that's right – Jessie still gets the same housekeeping – 30 bob!' Bob quipped, and the couple gave each other a warm smile. It perfectly captured a man happy in his own skin, and happy with his 'lot' – a lifetime in football.

Liverpool's Milk Cup clash with Manchester United was eagerly awaited – and for the third League Cup Final running, it went into extra time. Having been knocked out in the fifth round of the FA Cup by Brighton in February, Paisley knew the Milk Cup would be his last visit to Wembley in his capacity as Liverpool manager. And it turned out to be a very memorable afternoon for him. And in a truly unexpected way.

The match's main controversy happened when Bruce Grobbelaar ran 35 yards out of his goal to stop United's Gordon McQueen, by upending him. United claimed his rash decision should have been a sending-off offence – but it didn't happen, referee George Courtney seeing it only as a yellow card offence.

The goals? A 17-year-old Norman Whiteside scored a beauty in the 12th minute, and an equaliser for Liverpool came in the 75th minute, when that man Alan Kennedy added another to his exclusive collection of key goals, with a shot from outside the penalty area that beat the United keeper, Gary Bailey.

The match went into extra time, with the heavy pitch particularly affecting Ron Atkinson's men. The winning goal, his third in two consecutive League Cup finals, came from Irishman Ronnie Whelan in the 98th minute. He had spent a lot of the season out injured, but on this day at Wembley he crafted a brilliant goal, curving the ball around Bailey from just inside the left-hand side of the penalty area. Liverpool could have won by more, with substitute David Fairclough inexplicably missing three late chances.

At the end of the match, Liverpool captain Graeme Souness spoke to his manager Bob Paisley and, in a spontaneous gesture, invited him to lead the winning team up the 39 steps to the Royal Box to be presented with the Milk Cup. Bob didn't need much persuading, on this his final Wembley appearance as manager. He slipped off his smart raincoat and flat cap, and properly suited and booted took great pride on fulfilling something denied him many years ago. As Paisley climbed the stairs, somebody threw a Liverpool scarf across his left shoulder, then he picked up the trophy and lifted it up to the acclaim of his players and fans alike. A very special moment for all involved.

After the presentation, Bob joined the players on the pitch in front of the photographers – a set of outstanding footballers and a truly outstanding football manager.

Added Time:

- Joe Fagan was appointed the new Liverpool manager with a two-year contract on 1 July 1983 – once again the club had turned to the Boot Room to keep things moving smoothly on.

- On Saturday, 20 August, Liverpool and Manchester United met in the FA Charity Shield at Wembley, and, ahead of the game, two iconic club figures, Bob Paisley and Sir Matt Busby, were driven around in an open-roofed car to wave to the fans – in a public show of unity.
- Unlike their previous two matches in the Charity Shield, which had ended in draws, the 1983 encounter had a winner – Manchester United 2-0.
- As manager, Bob Paisley took Liverpool to Wembley 12 times. He lost only one of those games. In all his various roles at Liverpool, Paisley went to Wembley on an incredible 27 occasions.

***

Part Two: 'Merseyside, Merseyside, Merseyside'

1984

Merseyside had unfairly taken a major brunt of the effects of an economic and social downturn the country had found itself in during the early 80s. Its people had felt targeted by Margaret Thatcher's Government, with unemployment rife. It fell on the city's natural gift of looking after its own, and its huge talent in the fields of culture and sport to make sure that their corner was fought in eloquent, headline-grabbing and effective ways.

The BAFTA award-winning series *Boys from the Blackstuff* was a BBC TV five-part drama written by the Liverpool playwright Alan Bleasdale. It told the edgy, brittle story of a group of unemployed working-class Liverpool men who could see no hope, and no way out of their depths of despair, as their ability to find work and to provide for their loved ones collapsed around them. The series was such a seminal piece of work that after the tragi-comic drama's first run on BBC 2 in 1982, it was repeated in its entirety within nine weeks the following year on BBC1.

For many, the most talked-about episode featured that superb actor, the late Bernard Hill, who played the part of 'Yosser' Hughes, a man who felt he had lost everything – his job, his wife and potentially his three children – and his fall into mental turmoil was painful to watch. It included a cameo sequence when Hill's character found himself sitting alongside his famous 'lookalike', Graeme Souness, and teammate Sammy Lee.

'Gizza job' and 'I could do that' were phrases of desperation, manically used by Hill's character into the face of the Liverpool skipper. On the actor's death last year, Souness recalled that day spent with the acclaimed thespian: 'I remember sitting with Bernard having a coffee and him being very nice. But once the director asked us to start, within five seconds Bernard had turned into Yosser. And he became quite scary.'

If Bleasdale's drama was remarkably impactful, the city's other natural outlet, its football clubs, more than did their bit too – Liverpool and Everton and their respective supporters made sure their message of unity was heard loud and clear. And especially on one very special afternoon at Wembley. After years of near misses, with the two Merseyside clubs drawn against each other in major semi-finals rather than kept apart, the 1984 Milk Cup Final finally put that frustration to rest. Both teams had made it to a climax of the competition – a tremendous fillip for a city living under a cloud of depression and deprivation.

Sunday, 25 March 1984; Liverpool and Everton, two giants of English football, would meet head-on for the first time at Wembley in their respective illustrious histories. The build-up to the final started in February when both teams got through their two-legged semi-finals – Liverpool with

Walsall and Everton with Aston Villa. For the Reds it had been a marathon journey, involving 11 matches, involving a pair of two-legged affairs, Walsall and Brentford, a three-game tussle with Fulham, which the Reds crept through, two replayed ties with Birmingham City and Sheffield Wednesday.

Some of the attendances of the matches played at Anfield reflected a lack of interest in a competition Liverpool had now won three times – and the lack of spare money around. Brentford (9,902), Fulham (15,783), Birmingham City (11,638), Sheffield Wednesday (40,485) and Walsall (in the semi-final, 31,073). But the rush to get a ticket for the final itself was as mad as always.

Everton were about to hit their strides as a club after a long period in the doldrums. I was at the famous Oxford United/Everton fifth-round Milk Cup tie at the Manor Ground. Then owned by media mogul Robert Maxwell, Oxford were second in the Third Division (and would finish as champions), and already had the scalps of Leeds United, Newcastle United and Manchester United. They were leading Everton when a late goal from Adrian Heath via a misplaced pass by Oxford's Kevin Brock saved Howard Kendall's Blues from an embarrassing exit – and set them on the path to a remarkable run of success through the rest of the 80s.

Whatever else might have been ailing on Merseyside, football was back in the best of health. Everton only had Southampton standing in the way of another visit to Wembley for the FA Cup Final in May, while Joe Fagan's Liverpool had just heard they had drawn Dinamo Bucharest in the European Cup semi-final ahead of another possible European Cup Final in Rome. Everton's send-off from Merseyside included a kissogram girl waylaying Howard Kendall as he was about to board the coach – a stunt set up by full-back John Bailey.

Poems, songs, chants, banners – 'The Boys from The Blues Stuff', and a sense of togetherness. Red sitting with Blue, Blue drinking with Red. The match? It ended in a goalless draw after extra time. The main talking point? In the seventh minute, did the Reds' Alan Hansen handle the ball when intercepting a goalbound shot from Adrian Heath? While the referee, Alan Robinson, ignored the clamour, TV viewers at home, with the benefit of slow-motion replays, clearly saw the ball strike Hansen's thigh and then his left hand. No VAR in those days!

One interesting aside, when Everton substitute Alan Harper took over from Kevin Sheedy in the 75th minute, it instantly made Liverpool £30,000 richer. The second half of his transfer fee for his transfer from Anfield to Goodison became due because of his 30th appearance for the Blues. At the end of the game, both sets of players went up to the Royal Box to shake hands with the Queen Mother – and then back down on to the pitch.

There was an inspired joint lap of honour by the players. Spontaneously, echoing the camaraderie on the pitch, a crescendo began from the Wembley terraces and stands – 'Merseyside! Merseyside! Merseyside'. Time and again. That sound remains for those there – the indelible memory of the day the Blues painted the town red, and the Reds saw no reason to be blue.

Joe Fagan captured the mood perfectly: 'This was a day everyone should be proud of and I'm glad no one was a loser. Both sets of supporters were superb.'

He did, however, admit the Reds were not at the top of their game: 'What I said to the players at half-time is unprintable. Let's just say it was in industrial language which is best kept in the confines of the dressing room. The lads certainly did better in the second half but, overall, I am relieved with the result.'

Monday's newspapers were full of praise for the fans. 'There were no cups or medals handed out, but there was one winner – the unique sporting spirit, witnessed by a world-wide TV audience, brought to Wembley by Merseyside.'

Graeme Souness: 'It was a great occasion, a real advert for football and for Merseyside. I remember I got booked … met the Queen Mother … that was a nice moment. Deep down, though, we were happy we didn't lose, and we felt we couldn't do that badly again.'

The replay took place at Maine Road the following Wednesday, and a crowd of nearly 53,000 saw a brilliant goal by Liverpool captain Graeme Souness secure a narrow victory for the Reds – and the trophy itself, the Milk Cup became the permanent property of Liverpool Football Club. Liverpool would go on to win a treble: the European Cup, the First Division championship and the Milk Cup. A hugely significant achievement for the Anfield club. The free-scoring player of the year was Ian Rush, and that most modest of men, Joe Fagan, always a reluctant hero, was the manager of the year – another Boot Room success story.

It would also mark the end of Liverpool captain Graeme Souness's playing career at Anfield, after over 350 games. The stylish midfielder's ambition to play abroad ended with him signing for Italian club Sampdoria in the summer of 1984 before two years later becoming the player-manager at Glasgow Rangers – and a spell as Liverpool manager in the 1990s.

Howard Kendall and his Everton team returned to Wembley in May 1984 to win the FA Cup Final with a 2-0 victory over Elton John's Watford. 'I Guess That's Why They Call It the Blues.'

Added Time:

- Liverpool signed Danish midfielder Jan Mølby to fill the significant gap that the loss of Graeme Souness's departure would cause the Reds.
- Liverpool's 'reluctant boss' underlined one of the secrets of his team's success: 'Our methods are so easy sometimes players don't understand them at first.'

***

Part Three: Dalglish's Double

1986

If the 1984 'Merseyside' Milk Cup Final at Wembley Stadium was a marvellous spectacle in its own right, then the two great rivals and near-neighbours Everton and Liverpool meeting again in the 1986 FA Cup Final was on a different level again.

The cup final, the one the whole world annually tuned in for, was going to be graced by a derby match between Everton and Liverpool. The two outstanding English teams of the moment playing against each other at Pelé's 'Cathedral of Football' in the climax to the most important domestic cup competition in football. It would be their third meeting at Wembley in three years; the first had been the drawn match between the two sides in the Milk Cup Final, with no goals but tons of dignity and class shown on and off the pitch.

In the 1984 FA Charity Shield that summer, watched by another 100,000-capacity Wembley crowd, Everton came out on top as 1-0 winners, courtesy of a freakish Bruce Grobbelaar own goal.

The following season saw Everton crowned as English champions and winners in Europe too. For Liverpool, it was a season in which they finished runners-up in the league behind Howard Kendall's men, were beaten semi-finalists in the FA Cup and reached the European Cup Final, their fifth in nine years. Their opponents were Juventus, with the match to be played in the fated Heysel Stadium in Belgium.

Tragically, the ageing stadium was the scene of an horrendous tragedy when a pre-match charge by some Liverpool fans into a set of Italians and local people resulted in a wall collapsing, with the terrible outcome of the death of 39 people, the majority of them Italian, and a further 600 injured. The atmosphere in the stadium became febrile as the news of the fatalities filtered around the crowd – with the Italians fans justifiably angry and inflamed, and, although the match actually took place (Juventus won 1-0), it didn't really matter. After 21 seasons of unbroken European competition, Liverpool Football Club voluntarily withdrew from the following season's UEFA Cup, and more severe sanctions were imposed by UEFA on all English clubs – a five-year ban from European competition, with a further year added for the Anfield club.

There were many innocent victims that night of shame, not least a brilliant Everton team who, no doubt, would have done themselves proud in the European Cup the following season. Through no fault of their own, it was a missed opportunity. The resentment still lingers.

The 1985/86 season started with a new name in the manager's seat at Anfield – albeit a very familiar one. Joe Fagan was always going to step down at the end of his second season. The pictures of him in tears as he disembarked from the club's chartered flight from Brussels the morning after Heysel were heartbreaking.

Joe had done a tremendous job after taking over the reins from Bob Paisley but was realistic about what the future held for himself: 'I'm too old and tired. It's a job for a young man's brains and energy. It's not an eight-hours-a-day job. It's 24 hours a day. And there's no way you can get away from that.'

It had already leaked out that Kenny Dalglish, Liverpool's greatest-ever player, was going to combine his role on the field with the manager's job off it. And it was duly confirmed by Liverpool chairman, Sir John Smith, when Kenny Dalglish became Liverpool's first player-manager. And what followed is the stuff of legend.

Dalglish seemed a little cautious about his own self-selection in the early days of his new role – but even with Bob Paisley and Tom Saunders now adding their own helpful insight and advice, along with that of the Boot Room boys, Ronnie Moran and Roy Evans, the Scotsman was still very much his own man. He made Alan Hansen his new captain: 'First and foremost because he was a "very lucky person as well as a being a talented and respected footballer". If Al was sitting at 17 playing pontoon, he will get a four. It was the right decision.'

However, with Everton looking secure in the league's top spot after a convincing February win over the Reds at Anfield – eight points clear – Dalglish did what everybody wanted him to do. He picked his best player – himself. Liverpool went on a miraculous 12-game run – 11 wins and one draw – Dalglish playing in nine of the last 11.

Liverpool went top of the league on a 'Night of Destiny' late in the campaign. I was at Filbert Street with thousands of other Reds and watched LFC beat Leicester City 2-0. Subsequent news that Everton had gone down to a surprise late defeat at Oxford United was greeted with euphoria by the homeward-bound Liverpool supporters. Straightforwardly, if Liverpool won their final league game at Chelsea, they would be crowned champions. They duly won 1-0. The scorer? King Kenny, of course.

I was on duty at Stamford Bridge to try to get some post-match reaction to the Reds' title win for BBC's *Grandstand*.

Kenny Dalglish invited me into the dressing room where the players were rightfully celebrating their success. Kenny took off his shirt and playfully threw it at me. At the appropriate moment I decided to leave the Liverpool team to their hard-won privacy. And still clutching Kenny's sweat-drenched shirt, I said my goodbyes – only for Ronnie Moran, as matter of fact as always, league title win or no league title win, to shout over and say, 'Chuck that shirt in the kit basket on your way out. Cheers!' And I did. Reluctantly!

Liverpool were now on course, perhaps surprisingly, for a shot at winning the double. In the opposite corner, a wounded Everton team would be looking to square things up with a big win under the Twin Towers at the following weekend's FA Cup Final. Game on! In the days building up to the big day I was given the wonderful job of filming 'a week in the life' of an expectant city of Liverpool. It was a pinch-yourself moment (another one!) – in 1965, as a ten-year-old schoolboy, I had watched every minute of BBC's *Cup Final Grandstand*, not budging for five and a half hours, and now, in my role of Assistant Editor of BBC's flagship Saturday afternoon show, *Grandstand*, I was assigned to produce a 25-minute film to be broadcast in the opening half-hour of Saturday's big show.

No pressure then! I wanted it to be special – and to try to reflect the mood of a city so wrapped up in its football. Committed, devoted, fanatical, affectionate, witty, unique – Red and Blue. As much heart went into the film's production as did head. I laced the pictures with orchestral versions of Beatles music. The documentary literally romped along:

> Monday: Filming at Haydock races where Sammy Lee has a race named in his honour in this, his testimonial year, won by a horse called Mr Quick, which Lee generously accepts wouldn't have been named after him! Then it's off to Goodison Park

to watch Everton clinch second place in the league with a win over West Ham – and Gary Lineker picks up his PFA Player of the Year award.

Tuesday: A crowd of 26,696 gather at Anfield to see Liverpool beat Norwich City in the Screen Sport Super Cup semi-final – but really come to watch the Liverpool team receive the Canon League Trophy. The Kop is ecstatic.

Wednesday: We drop in to Liverpool Maternity Hospital to take some beautiful footage of proud new parents Craig Johnston and his wife Jenny, and their brand-new baby, six-day-old Cassie. Craig would score a goal for her in Saturday's final.

Thursday: It's local election day in Liverpool when the colours, red and blue, relate to another important aspect of British life. We get socialist firebrand and Toffees fanatic Deputy Mayor Derek Hatton, to wish both Blues and Reds a good day on Saturday … and then leave quickly.

Elsewhere, Lineker receives his FWA Footballer of the Year award, and popular BBC Radio Merseyside DJ Billy Butler shows his impartiality by playing the two clubs' 'Cup Final' records – Liverpool's 'Sitting on Top of the World' and Everton's 'Everybody's Cheering the Blues' on his show – simultaneously!

Friday: Everton's Howard Kendall sportingly presents the manager of the year award to Kenny Dalglish. Elsewhere, Rev. Harry Ross, vicar of St Luke's Church at the corner of Goodison Park, and a devout Evertonian, prays that everything

> will go well this week for Merseyside. His church has only three things in red: carpets that are walked on, hassocks that are knelt on and seats that are sat on! The church bells ring out on Friday evening, and the camera beautifully catches a late spring sun setting and weaving patterns on the sparkling water beneath it, as an iconic lone ferry slowly crosses the River Mersey.
>
> Saturday: It's early morning, the Wembley football specials spill out of Lime Street Station with red- and blue-decked supporters sharing bacon sandwiches and good-natured banter. Then there was a massive 40-a-side Reds vs Blues friendly match being played in the car park near the stadium, with the classic 'jumpers for goalposts'.

It's cup final day! My own cup final morning started at Liverpool's hotel from where I sent up-to-date pictures of the players relaxing ahead of the afternoon's exertions to insert into BBC's *Cup Final Grandstand* coverage – and we followed behind the team coach, filming its journey to Wembley Stadium. Once the players had reached the dressing room area, my job was all but done and my *Grandstand* bosses kindly let me off for the rest of the day, so I was able to meet up with some mates and watch the final in the way I best loved – as a fan.

Kenny Dalglish had waited until he and his players were in the Wembley dressing room before he announced the actual line-up for that afternoon's big game. Kenny explained his thinking behind what, to many, would seem to have been a late call: 'When we arrived at the stadium, the squad didn't know who would be playing. We'd had the additional problem that Gary Gillespie hadn't fully recovered from a virus that had troubled him for a couple of days. I talked to various people about the selection but, in the end, it was my decision. That's the way it always has to be.'

And here is that team: Grobbelaar; Nicol, Hansen, Lawrenson, Beglin; Johnston, Macdonald, Mølby, Whelan; Dalglish, Rush. Sub: McMahon. The starting line-up was the first in an FA Cup Final without an Englishman in it – Mark Lawrenson, though born in Preston, having represented the Republic of Ireland at international level. Indeed, the starting XI had no Scouser in it either. It was a team shaped and modelled by Dalglish, and it took to the field destined to make football history.

In truth, the Reds looked second best in the first half at Wembley, and Everton led through a Gary Lineker goal. Dalglish told his players at half-time: 'We've been magnificent all season, there's 45 minutes to go and give it our lot.'

And they did. The Great Dane, Jan Mølby, took charge of the midfield, and it was his pass in the 57th minute that found Ian Rush, who sidestepped Everton's goalkeeper, Bobby Mimms and levelled the scores. Six minutes later Rush returned the compliment with a pass that Mølby turned across goal, marginally ahead of Dalglish, but into the path of Aussie, Craig Johnston. A truly international goal – a Welshman, a Dane and an Aussie – 2-1. The clincher came in the 84th minute, when a Mølby pass found Ronnie Whelan, whose floated centre landed perfectly for Rush to nail his second goal, and Liverpool's third, 3-1.

The double had been achieved in Dalglish's first season in the manager's seat – a remarkable achievement. And his own assessment of key moments and men at Wembley were typically insightful. Back on Merseyside, the fabled *Football Echo* roared out its Saturday evening headline – 'KENNY'S KINGS DOUBLE TOP'.

The following afternoon I joined both teams at Heathrow Airport to travel on a shared British Airways Boeing 757 back to Liverpool's Speke Airport.

It had probably seemed a good idea when it was booked several weeks before, but for the Everton players, pipped at the post by their fiercest rivals twice within eight days, it must have been tough. Indeed, Peter Reid ducked out and made his own way home. All was calm on board the plane, and both teams were welcomed home by hundreds of thousands of people – Red and Blue – a city immensely proud of its football clubs.

Dalglish: 'The scenes on the journey around the city were unbelievable. Both sets of supporters were out, thousands and thousands, red and blue everywhere you looked.'

I was on board the Liverpool bus grabbing interviews as it made its way around the city, a real experience on its own, but paused in that work as it got close to Childwall Fiveways, a major roundabout system near my old family home. I knew that would be where my mother would be standing at the roadside – that's where she always stood for the homecomings – red or blue.

Sure enough, I spotted her, and, as I did, Kenny Dalglish mischievously pushed me to the front of the bus, where, among others, I briefly had the FA Cup itself as a travelling companion. Totally unprofessional. And absolutely memorable.

Added Time:

- Liverpool and Everton met again in August in the FA Charity Shield in front of 88,000 fans at Wembley. This time, the match ended in a 1-1 draw.
- The two clubs met no less than six times during the season – the FA Charity Shield, two league matches, a Football League Cup tie and in the two-legged Screen

Sport Super Cup Final – the Reds won four of those games, drew two and lost none.

- In the 1986/87 season, Ian Rush scored *nine* goals against Everton, having scored two of the goals in the win over Everton in the FA Cup Final in the previous season.
- Ian Rush would sign for Juventus at the end of the 1986/87 season – John Aldridge had been signed as his replacement.

***

Part Four: A Proper Charlie and the Crazy Gang

1987

Going into the 1987 Football League Cup Final against Arsenal at Wembley, one thing was for sure. If Ian Rush scored, Liverpool would win.

That was the theory anyway. Rushie's scoring prowess was unrivalled and, in what would be his last season with the Reds, well, before the next one … after a year in Italy … a goal from the Welsh wizard invariably tied things up for Liverpool. 144 times … 144 times! Incredibly, Liverpool had never lost a game in which Ian Rush scored. A simply unbelievable record and one that his team-mates had just come to expect – match in, match out.

En route to the 5 April final – now called the Littlewoods Challenge Cup Final for sponsorship reasons – the Reds had enjoyed a couple of special wins. They won 10-0 in the first leg of their second-round tie with Fulham on a wet and windy night at Anfield. Rush scored twice, but the star of the evening was Steve McMahon, who scored four in this landslide victory. He also scored in the Reds' 3-2 win in the second leg at Craven Cottage. Aggregate score 13-2 to the Reds. And an Ian

Rush goal at Goodison Park, against their near-neighbours, gave Liverpool a passage into the semi-finals, where they comprehensively dealt with opponents Southampton.

And so, to Wembley – again – for the Reds' sixth tilt in ten seasons at the English football's 'second' cup competition, not bad for a club that had given the whole thing a huge swerve in its formative years.

Kenny Dalglish's starting line-up for this game showed five changes from his 1986 FA Cup Final selection. Barry Venison, Nigel Spackman, Gary Gillespie, Steve McMahon and Paul Walsh came in against the Gunners. In the opposition line-up, a player that the Anfield club had been attracted to themselves. Certainly, at one point, Joe Fagan and the club's Scottish contingent had made sure that Charlie Nicholas knew he might have a splendid future at LFC. However, despite their interest, and that of Manchester United, the young Glaswegian, who had become a folk hero at Celtic, plumped for Arsenal and a life in the bright lights of the capital.

He perhaps thought he wouldn't be guaranteed a regular game with Liverpool, given the strength of the Anfield squad, but that might have worked in his favour in helping him to settle more naturally into the pace and intensity of the premier division in English football. Playing Charlie Nicholas up front alongside Rush with Dalglish working his magic just behind them might have worked a treat – but it wasn't to be.

It would prove over time, not to fully work out at Highbury for the Scottish lad heralded on his arrival as the new 'wonder boy' but on this Sunday afternoon at a sun-kissed Wembley, Charlie was the real deal – a 'proper Charlie'. He scored twice, both goals having an element of luck about them, but he won the game for Arsenal – even after Ian Rush had scored the match's opener with all the expectation that went with it.

Rush would head off to Italy at the end of the season and fittingly scored in the club's final home game against Watford. And the Kop gave him a very warm goodbye.

1988

Wimbledon is a word synonymous with the English summer: strawberries and cream, a glass of Pimm's, hot and late June afternoons, the 'oohs and aahs' of the Centre Court crowd, the patriotic support on Henman Hill and Murray Mound, the beautifully tended grass courts and the very best tennis players in the world fighting it out to join the legendary names that have gone before them.

In 1988, it would be Sweden's Stefan Edberg who would beat Boris Becker to take the men's crown, while Becker's German compatriot, Steffi Graf, started her route to women's tennis domination by beating another sporting icon, Martina Navratilova, to win her first Wimbledon title. So, all things SW19 in order.

However, earlier in the year, the name Wimbledon was seen in a different sporting context with a famous unlikely victory on a very special day at Wembley Stadium. And their brief flash of fame went global.

The year of 1988 saw the first Red Nose Day – it raised £15 million for Comic Relief, which had begun its own life in 1985, and the charity has gone on to raise £1 billion to help disadvantaged people the world over – and nearer to home.

It was also the year that saw the end of the pound note, Health Minister Edwina Currie lost her job after creating an egg/salmonella drama, and 270 people died when a Pan Am aircraft exploded over Lockerbie in Scotland – the victims of an outrageous terrorist act.

Closer to home in Liverpool, Prince Charles opened the newly renovated Albert Dock (now the Royal Albert

Dock) as a leisure and business centre in Liverpool. In the last quarter of a century, it has been visited by four million people annually and is the most visited multiuse attraction in the UK outside of London. A huge and most welcome boost for the Merseyside economy.

On the football scene, the two Merseyside clubs were still ruling the roost. Kenny Dalglish's men were crowned league champions for the 17th time – and one of their wins, a midweek 5-0 thrashing of Brian Clough's Nottingham Forest, just four days after they had also beaten them in the FA Cup semi-final, brought high praise indeed. The great Tom Finney declared: 'They must be the best of all time. That was the finest exhibition by any team in all my time of playing and watching the game.'

Equally impressed was a major international football figure, Michel Platini: 'In replacing Ian Rush with Peter Beardsley, John Barnes and John Aldridge they have traded one great player for three more great players.'

Liverpool's second double seemed a distinct possibility as their opponents in the 1998 FA Cup Final would be Wimbledon FC. Unfashionable, quirky, unique – the Dons of Plough Lane had defied the odds time and again in their rapid rise from non-league football to the top half of the top league in the land, English football's First Division. Yet the nation was clearly expecting Liverpool to win the final and win it comfortably – and even considered that a victory for the South London side would be considered an FA Cup giant-killing.

I never bought that. After all, the Dons finished seventh in the First Division, not too shabby, and had held Liverpool to a 1-1 draw at Plough Lane that season. Living in London at this time, I regularly went to see the football clubs that played in the capital – and such was the warm welcome I got whenever I went there that I frequently went to see

Wimbledon at their ramshackle ground at Plough Lane. It had a 16,000 capacity, the club's chairman, Stanley Reed, was a wonderful old English gentleman, and his sidekick was an eccentric Lebanese businessman called Sam Hammam, who relentlessly drove the club forward.

Former player Dave Bassett was the manager and had got the club up through the divisions – and when he left to manage Watford, the experienced Bobby Gould took over the reins. And he was astute enough to hire Don Howe, a coaching guru, as his chief support.

Having watched a lot of Wimbledon matches, I knew they were no pushovers, their style of play was uncompromising, they fancied hitting the ball long on any, or every, occasion, and made no apologies for making the life of the visiting team horrible both on and off the pitch. With martial arts expert John Fashanu up front, Dennis 'The Menace' Wise on the wing, Dave Beasant in goal, Lawrie Sanchez and Alan Cork, experienced men, and former hod carrier Vinnie Jones in midfield, they had a fascinating mix of brain and brawn.

Vinnie Jones had come off the building site and a role in part-time football at Wealdstone to go full-time with the Dons, less than two years before their big day at Wembley. He had already made a big impression on English football – not least because of his ferocious tackling and his 'up and at 'em' attitude. He was a key part of the inner spirit of the Wimbledon side.

Of course, the media and the public alike waited in anticipation for the moment when tough nut Vinnie met the elegant Princess Diana, the FA Cup Final's royal guest, as she was introduced to the two teams before the match that day. And they weren't disappointed.

Liverpool had prepared properly for the big Wembley game. Indeed, their cup final record, 'The Anfield Rap', had reached the dizzy heights of number three in the charts. Wimbledon were determined to unsettle them – and there is a well-worn theory that they looked to spook Liverpool with verbal abuse as the teams lined up in the tunnel. Those who wore the red shirts that day debunk the story, saying it never happened.

The match itself turned on three key incidents. Firstly, Liverpool's Peter Beardsley had a goal disallowed by referee Brian Hill, who brought the game back for a free kick to Liverpool. A minute later came the only goal of the game. The Dons' diminutive winger, Dennis Wise, floated a free kick into the Reds' penalty area and Lawrie Sanchez deftly headed home. Midweek head injuries to Reds Gary Gillespie and Nigel Spackman somewhat hampered those two players, especially playing against a team of six-footers.

Into the second half, and Liverpool applied a champion's pressure. Wimbledon resisted bravely until Clive Goodyear upended John Aldridge in the box. A penalty, albeit a soft one. Aldridge got up and took the penalty himself but the Dons keeper and captain, Dave Beasant, had done his homework and guessed right to save brilliantly. It was the first penalty saved in an FA Cup Final and Beasant became the first goalkeeper to lift the famous trophy.

It was a famous victory, made headline news and denied Liverpool a second double. Dalglish's reaction to the defeat was typically honest and to the point: 'The simple reason why Wimbledon won the game was because they took their chance and Liverpool didn't.'

Added Time:

- Three days after winning the final, the Wimbledon players were filmed 'mooning' at the end of Alan Cork's testimonial match. The FA were not 'over the moon' about the incident and charged them!

- Liverpool had actually played at Wembley in the month before the 1988 FA Cup Final as part of the Football League's 100th anniversary of their founding. In a poorly supported two-day event – the Football League Centenary Tournament – 16 clubs were invited to play in a series of 40-minute-long matches – Liverpool drew 0-0 with Newcastle United in the opening round and went out of the competition on penalties – and swiftly headed back home!
- In August's FA Charity Shield, Liverpool beat Wimbledon 2-1. John Aldridge scored both Liverpool goals after Fashanu had opened the scoring for the Dons.
- In the same month, Ian Rush returned to Liverpool from Juventus.

* * *

Part Five: Merseyside United

1989

The Hillsborough disaster was the darkest day in English football, when 97 Liverpool fans lost their lives for just going to watch a football match.

It remains an unbelievably sad fact that those supporters who had attended the FA Cup semi-final against Nottingham Forest at Sheffield Wednesday's Hillsborough Stadium were lost to their loved ones forever. The fight for justice for those who died has been long and deeply frustrating – but it is now clear that the people crushed to death at the stadium's Leppings Lane end were the innocent victims of poor decision-making by the senior officers in charge of operations that day – and efforts to cover up those fatally flawed decisions.

Liverpool Football Club, the city of Liverpool itself and football in general were at the centre of a huge outpouring of grief. Indeed, the pitch at Anfield became a sea of flowers spreading from and on the Kop down to the halfway line. It became a shrine to those who had lost their lives.

I went myself and laid flowers on behalf of my colleagues at BBC Sport – and was then invited in to see Kenny Dalglish and his players, still shocked by the previous Saturday's tragic happenings but all keen to be available to speak or listen to friends and relatives of those who had died or been seriously injured.

The previous Saturday I'd had to find a way of reporting the affairs of that afternoon in a *Match of the Day* edition with essentially no football in it. I was determined to keep our programme in the BBC TV schedule because we were a trusted football programme and our audience would naturally be those most upset and affected by the tragedy at Hillsborough – and *Match of the Day*'s senior presenter, Desmond Lynam, and the vastly experienced Jimmy Hill had actually been at that stadium itself on the afternoon, and then rushed back to London to describe what they had seen and what they felt.

I produced hundreds of TV programmes in my time at BBC TV, but none was more important than the one we produced that evening.

***

And after a profound and deep level of mourning, Liverpool FC finally got down to playing football again, their first match an emotional friendly at Celtic, and their first competitive match against Everton.

The Everton fans had been brilliant in supporting their Red 'brothers and sisters' during the difficult time between the abandoned semi-final and this rescheduled derby match (and always have been), and it just seemed right that Kenny Dalglish's men should pick up the pieces again just over the park at Goodison Park. The match played on 3 May ended goalless as a subsequent special FA Cup Final *Liverpool Echo* tastefully reflected.

Just 27 days later the two great Merseyside clubs would meet again in the 1989 FA Cup Final at Wembley Stadium. It would be an occasion that would duly pay its respect for those victims of the tragedy and their bereaved family and friends.

'Togetherness is the key here today … these pictures are being beamed across the world to the United States of America, Hungary and Iraq … indeed, to all countries that normally tune in for the FA Cup Final. They will all appreciate this year is different.' The opening words of the late John Motson in his commentary for BBC TV's coverage of the 1989 FA Cup Final.

It was different – fences came down and supporters were allowed to sit on the outskirts of the pitch. Gerry Marsden led the whole crowd in an emotional rendition of 'You'll Never Walk Alone', and a minute's silence was perfectly observed for the Hillsborough victims.

The game itself was a fitting memorial to those lost – football fans – because it was a match brimming with exciting football, marvellous goals and plenty of twists and turns. Liverpool went ahead after just four minutes when a pair of Scousers, Steve McMahon and John Aldridge, combined to allow the man who had missed a penalty in the final the previous year to score a brilliant goal.

The game was in its closing moments when Blues' substitute Stuart McCall scrambled a late equaliser. Into extra time, and Liverpool's own substitute, Ian Rush, turned in a virtuoso display of finishing. He put Liverpool ahead, only to see Stuart McCall hit an unlikely and brilliant equaliser – again.

Finally, the game's fifth and decisive goal. John Barnes crossed from the left and Ian Rush guided a header with marvellous precision into the back of the Everton net. Ronnie Whelan lifted the FA Cup, and the Liverpool team went on a lap of honour punctuated with celebrating fans, many of whom had surrounded the pitch.

After the match, I left Wembley Stadium and hastily made my way to the BBC TV Studios to put together that night's edition of *Match of the Day*. Along with highlights of the match, post-match interviews and pundits' analysis, we ended the programme with a beautifully crafted montage of pictures of the day to the music of 'Ferry Across the Mersey', which we hoped reflected the unity of spirit on a very special day at Wembley.

A few days later I received a letter from Bill Kenwright, Everton fanatic, board member and future long-time chairman of Everton, and West End theatrical impresario. It read:

> I sat watching the video of Match of the Day yesterday and after re-living it all over again, I decided that my time in front of the television set was pure masochism, and a big mistake!! However, your ending collage of 'Ferry Across the Mersey' came on and I sat weeping buckets! More than anything else, it summed up the weekend for me, and I simply wanted to tell you and your colleagues it was brilliant, and I will keep it forever.

It was fitting that Liverpool had won the final. Six days later they had a domestic double ripped away from them with a last-second Michael Thomas goal for the resulting champions, Arsenal. Disappointing? Yes, but in the context of what the club and its supporters had suffered just weeks before, it was just a sporting result, not a matter of life or death.

Added Time:

- Michael Thomas scored the goal that robbed Liverpool of the double but in 1992, now a Liverpool player, he scored a stunning goal for the Reds in the club's 2-0 FA Cup Final win over Sunderland.
- Having played each other in the last match of the 1988/89 season in late May, Liverpool met Arsenal twice in a matter of weeks at Wembley ahead of the new 1989/90 season.
- In the last weekend of July, Liverpool lost to Arsenal in the final of the Makita International Tournament, having beaten Dynamo Kiev at Wembley the previous afternoon.
- Just a fortnight later the FA Charity Shield was won by Liverpool with a Peter Beardsley goal against League champions, Arsenal. The relatively low Wembley crowd of 63,149 suggested that there was a little bit of overkill.

Chapter 5

1990s: And Then the Cupboard Was …?

Part One: 'And the Times, They Are a-Changing …'

The 1990s in the UK would see a significant shift in power. In politics and in football. It would be the decade when Labour's Tony Blair was handed the keys to 10 Downing Street after 18 years of Conservative rule. 'Things Can Only Get Better' rang out around Whitehall.

Meanwhile, in the same decade, staunch Labour man, Manchester United manager Alex Ferguson was determined to knock his chief rivals down the M62, Liverpool, 'off their bloody perch'. The Merseyside Reds had ruled the roost in English and European football since the mid-70s; trophy after trophy, title after title, final after final.

Shankly had passed the baton to Paisley, Paisley to Fagan, Fagan to Dalglish. Liverpool were simply a winning machine – the first whistle of the new season always more important than the last blast of the previous campaign. Always look forwards not backwards. They knew how to enjoy their successes, but the Boot Room would soon get everybody's heads turned to the future. But if things were about to change on the pitch, then important things were happening off it as well.

By August 1992, the Football League's First Division had dissolved into the Premiership. Satellite TV money, chiefly Rupert Murdoch's Sky TV money, did all the talking needed and the consequences reached of that money-spinning gamble spread far and wide – the footballing landscape was about to change forever.

Not a bad time to get your act together at Old Trafford, and an inopportune time for Liverpool to lose their mojo – their finest player turned manager – and while remaining a huge name in the sport but without the baubles that went with it. It is remarkable to think that in the 15 seasons from 1975/76 to 1989/90, Liverpool won four European Cups, one UEFA Cup, one European Super Cup, ten league championships, two FA Cups and four Football League Cups. They were the top dogs. No mistaking that.

Conversely, in the first ten years of the FA Premier League, to give it its original title, which started in 1992/93, Manchester United won the title on no less than seven occasions, having previously not won the league title since 1967. The signs of a power switch had been there at the very start of the decade.

Liverpool won the league title, again, and looked on course to land the double. However, in an exhilarating and dramatic FA Cup semi-final at Villa Park, Liverpool gave up a 3-2 lead late in the game to ultimately lose 4-3 in extra time to Crystal Palace. Palace's manager, Steve Coppell, that day was a former Kopite, and he was a friend and colleague of mine during our schooldays together at Quarry Bank High School and later at the University of Liverpool. Steve had earlier in the season suffered a humiliating 9-0 league defeat at the hands of Kenny Dalglish's men – and a further 2-0 league defeat at Selhurst Park. Coppell: 'After losing 9-0 and 2-0 in the league, I would have been happy with just 1-0. To get four goals against the best team in the country renews your faith in our players and everything they do.' Despite my natural allegiance for the Reds, I was quietly chuffed for Steve.

On the same afternoon, Manchester United survived a scare in their FA Cup semi-final – 3-3 against Oldham Athletic at Maine Road – and went on to win the replay. Famously, they had also survived an early exit from the competition when they defeated Nottingham Forest. Mark Robins's late goal saved Alex Ferguson's bacon – or so legend has it. Manchester United won a replayed FA Cup Final against Crystal Palace, the first match 3-3, the replay 1-0 (Lee Martin) – and Fergie's United were off and running.

Meanwhile, Liverpool celebrated their 11th title in 18 seasons, and whether us fans were becoming a bit complacent about it all, incredibly it would be the club's last title success for the next 30 years.

The two successful teams came together in the 68th FA Charity Shield at Wembley in front of a 66,558 crowd – Liverpool as league champions and Manchester United as FA Cup winners. On the day, manager Kenny Dalglish stepped aside and invited long-serving stalwart of the club Ronnie Moran to have the honour of leading out Liverpool at Wembley. The match ended in a 1-1 draw, Clayton Blackmore scoring for United, John Barnes equalising from the spot in the second half. Both clubs held the trophy for six months.

Interestingly, in a curtain-raiser before the big game, England's women played an international against their Italian counterparts. England lost 4-1 but the ball was rolling.

* * *

The 1990s were considered a decade where exciting possibilities were opening up for people, although it wasn't all glee, as there were still economic issues, including the country facing a recession in the early part of the decade. There was a rise in multiculturalism, the 'tech' bubble would explode late in the decade, and a new form of laughter-makers, alternative comedians, who ironically became the norm.

By the end of the decade we were all using the internet, texting each other, buying books from Amazon, playing the National Lottery and using Google to make sure we were fully armed and ready with all the answers for the weekly pub quiz. 'Cool Britannia' was encapsulated in the music of Blur and Oasis – and the Spice Girls became the most talked-about girl band ever.

Del Boy was still making Rodney look a right 'plonker' as BBC's hit comedy *Only Fools and Horses* continued to deliver huge viewing figures – and episodes of *Friends* were doing the same in the US. And it's still watched the world over to this day. In the cinema we all hoped 'My Heart Would Go On' as *Titanic* was the decade's box-office smash hit. The top-selling album of the decade in the UK would be Oasis's massive *(What's the Story) Morning Glory?*

On a more sombre note, the Gulf War got underway in 1990, UK troops joining their American counterparts and the coalition's armed forces to defeat Saddam Hussein. And, later in the decade, on 31 August 1997, Diana, the Princess of Wales, was tragically killed in a car crash in the Pont de l'Alma tunnel in Paris. Others fatally injured in the crash were her companion, Dodi Fayed, and the driver of the Mercedes-Benz, Henri Paul. Her death was mourned the world over.

* * *

On Merseyside there had been a seismic shock of a different nature in February 1991 when Kenny Dalglish resigned his position as manager of Liverpool. Two days after drawing 4-4 in an FA Cup replay with neighbours+ Everton, a press conference was hastily called at Anfield where the club's greatest player, successful manager and special human being, given the hours he spent with those most affected by the Hillsborough disaster, confirmed he was leaving the club.

He and his wife, Marina, had done their brilliant best from the moment the Hillsborough disaster took place. For once, now he put his own health and his family first and stepped away from the game.

After a short period with Ronnie Moran taking the managerial reins in a caretaker capacity, the Anfield club appointed another Liverpool legend, Graeme Souness, as their new manager. With a playing record of over 350 games with the Reds, an influential club captain and serial winner, the Scotsman looked a perfect choice to replace his former team-mate and great friend, Kenny Dalglish. Souness had enjoyed his spell in Italy playing for Sampdoria and then had a hugely positive impact as manager of Glasgow Rangers. What could go wrong?

Part Two: A Century … and a Cup

In 1992, Liverpool Football Club was celebrating its Centenary – 100 years of a club that had grown from modest beginnings to now become one of the most famous sporting institutions in the world.

Liverpool's league performances under the new manager in his first full season were flaky, finishing a disappointing sixth, but everybody hoped that the club's centenary year would be blessed with a trophy. The 1991/92 FA Cup competition would prove to be the delivery mechanism by which that ambition was achieved. But there were plenty of bumps along the way.

In recent times, the FA Cup has lost a little of its lustre, with the all-pervading Premier League and ultra-marketed UEFA Champions League taking much, if not all, of the big boys' strong focus and attention – and, in the case of the Premier League, the smaller clubs' determination to stay in it and enjoy the huge financial windfall that comes with it. Premier League clubs have fielded weakened teams in the post-Christmas early rounds – and even Championship clubs, with aspirations of reaching the Premier League's golden pastures, have also followed suit.

The removal of replays has also stripped away some of the competition's great romance too. The competition can still provide a great 'upset' and back-page headline, and the FA Cup Final is still a phenomenally important part of the English football's domestic calendar – and should be cherished. It remains the most revered domestic cup competition in world football.

In the 1991/92 FA Cup, the unique beauty and sheer breadth of the competition was illustrated as it got underway on 31 August when 308 clubs entered the preliminary round. The smallest attendance of the 154 ties played that day was at the Molesey vs Ringmer match, which attracted the grand total of just 25 fans. Nine months later, Liverpool would meet Sunderland in the FA Cup Final in front of a crowd of nearly 80,000 fans at Wembley Stadium, and with simply millions of TV viewers watching it worldwide, at whatever time of day or night it was where they were lived. Such was the annual attraction of the FA Cup Final.

Liverpool's route to the final was not straightforward. A 4-0 win at Crewe in the third round was followed by a 2-1 replay win over Bristol Rovers in the next stage of the competition. A 3-2 home win over Ipswich Town took them through to the quarter-finals, where a single goal from Michael Thomas, the man who had clinched the title for Arsenal at Anfield three years earlier, was enough to knock out Aston Villa. It was at the FA Cup semi-final stage that things got sticky for Liverpool.

Playing second-tier Portsmouth at Highbury, the Reds trailed to a 111th-minute Darren Anderton goal, before a Ronnie Whelan strike five minutes later took the tie to a replay. A short time after the Highbury game, Graeme Souness was admitted to hospital to have a triple-heart bypass operation, which he had been aware he was going to have to face ahead of the Highbury semi-final. Souness initially got through the prolonged operation safely, but a dangerous infection set in and the Liverpool boss became very unwell, and his stay in hospital lasted for 28 days.

During that period, *The Sun* carried an exclusive interview with the Liverpool manager during his convalescence, which was printed together with a photo in the paper on the day of the Hillsborough anniversary. It is believed to have been published a day later than originally intended because Liverpool's replay with Portsmouth had gone into extra time and penalties – with the Reds ultimately clinching a Wembley cup final place. The whole affair soured Souness's relationship with the Liverpool supporters – he subsequently recognised he had made a regrettable mistake.

Souness had only been out of hospital a few days when, to show solidarity with the club, its players and supporters, he attended the FA Cup Final against Sunderland at a rainy Wembley Stadium. I had gone to the club's pre-cup final base in St Albans the day before the match and had a few words with the Liverpool manager. He looked tired and drawn, as anybody who had gone through his medical ordeal would have done.

On 6 April 1992, Ronnie Moran had taken up the caretaker-manager reins and responsibilities when Graeme Souness had his extended stay in hospital. A mixed set of results in the league followed but the penalty shoot-out win against Portsmouth – Dean Saunders scoring the crucial kick – meant Moran would now be preparing the Liverpool team for the FA Cup Final against Sunderland, who, themselves, would also be led out by a rookie boss, Malcolm Crosby.

Souness was at the match but, still convalescing, was unable to fulfil all the duties of a manager on the day. He was flanked on the bench by club doctor Bill Reid and Liverpool physio Paul Chadwick, so it fell to the smartly dressed Ronnie Moran to lead the Reds out of the tunnel again at Wembley – this time in a suit! 'It was a very proud moment for me,' confirmed Moran, who then settled into his business gear – his tracksuit!

My own role on the big day? Thirty years on from watching my first FA Cup Final back in 1962, I was now one of the key editorial figures working on BBC TV's live coverage of the match. I was at Wembley – or, to be more precise, right outside the stadium, in one of the main BBC Television's outside broadcast trucks – scanners – helping drive the BBC's programme content and studio discussions and analysis, pre-match, at half-time and post-match. In another truck, a vastly experienced match director, John Shrewsbury, would be responsible for producing the live pictures of the game itself.

A BBC army of over 150 people would be working on the game in their various capacities – relying on each other to get their bit right to give the viewer the best possible coverage of this major sporting event. The UK TV audience for the final would be around 15 million, but something like 500 million across the globe.

I did get nervous on these 'big telly' days, but then your own experience and know-how kicked in – and off we went, and you always knew you were surrounded by a team of gifted individuals. Once in the TV van, it was business as usual. Even if Liverpool were in the final!

Liverpool won – no classic – with two second-half goals – a blinder from Michael Thomas and a clincher from

Ian Rush – his fifth FA Cup Final goal. A young Steve McManaman made a huge impression that afternoon on a Wembley pitch he would grace again – and again. He later played this tribute to Moran: 'Anything he said was never too complicated and he made it sound as simple as possible. As far as I'm concerned, they are the best instructions you can ever get as a player.'

So, Liverpool had won a trophy in their centenary year – and the players got their winners' medals – eventually! Captain Mark Wright lifted the trophy, but the presentation of the medals went a little wrong! The beaten Sunderland players looked at their medals inscribed with 'FA Cup Winner 1992' – then realised the Liverpool players had been given the runners-up medals. Swaps took place on the pitch and the mishap was quickly corrected. Thankfully.

In August 1992, Liverpool were back at Wembley Stadium for the FA Charity Shield match against the First Division champions, Leeds United. In a free-scoring game, Howard Wilkinson's Leeds United came out on top, winning 4-3, with an enigmatic Frenchman called Eric Cantona scoring a hat-trick.

Temperamental and brilliant, Cantona would go on to become a regular thorn in Liverpool's side after he moved across the Pennines and joined Alex Ferguson's Manchester United – the final piece in the jigsaw. Not least, at Wembley again, when he scored the winning goal in the 1996 FA Cup Final. More on that to come.

Part Three: Super Steve's Showpiece Show!

Leeds United had been the last winners of the Football League First Division championship as the 1992/93 season was about to start its 'Whole New Ball Game' on Sky Sports with live coverage of the newly branded Premier League. Essentially, the same competition as before but with knobs on – but with a remarkable future lying ahead of it.

I had spent the whole of the previous year 'keeping close' to Rick Parry, the CEO of the new Premier League; later, of course, the CEO of Liverpool Football Club, and now the EFL (English Football League) chairman. I found Rick to be a decent guy to deal with, and the fact that he also supported Liverpool was not unhelpful.

The BBC knew that the big bucks needed to secure live Premier League matches would be out of the licence fee's reach but were determined to keep its prized asset *Match of the Day* intact, and I was given the task of making sure our determination to keep the iconic highlights show in the BBC1's much-prized Saturday night schedule was secured by winning those broadcast rights. We made our case in football circles – and especially in the office of the Premier League's new CEO. That was my job.

The number of viewers (or subscribers!) able to watch the matches live on Sky was still relatively small at this point, so a well-established programme like *Match of the Day* served its purpose – and took some of the heat off the satellite broadcasters and the clubs who had voted to go on a whole new, and well-funded, broadcast journey. This was a venture that wouldn't be universally approved by the fans, but the status and fame of the competition that has subsequently followed cannot be denied.

The BBC duly won the rights to retain their famous Saturday night slot of top football action – and Liverpool FC would make more TV sport broadcasting history. Their match on the opening day of the season against Arsenal at Anfield in August 1964 had kickstarted the life of *Match of the Day* on the newly created BBC2, and now the Reds were featured in the first live Premier League match on Sky – a 1-0 defeat at Nottingham Forest.

***

We spin forward to April 1995 – and Liverpool's next big occasion at Wembley Stadium – the Coca-Cola Cup Final against Bolton Wanderers. But not before registering the closure of one of the most legendary sights and structures in sport. If Wembley Stadium would have its famous overhaul in the first decade of the new century, then the closing of the Kop at Anfield, from being the most famous terrace in football to a safer environment of seating following the tragedy of five years before at Hillsborough, also made huge news.

On its final day, the Liverpool legends came out of the players' tunnel, cheered to the rafters by the adoring Anfield crowd. Great names – heroes all – Albert Stubbins, Billy Liddell, Ian Callaghan, Tommy Smith, Steve Heighway, David Johnston, David Fairclough, Craig Johnston, ex-Kopite Phil Thompson and the club's greatest-ever player, Kenny Dalglish.

Then, to a resounding standing ovation, former manager Joe Fagan emerged from the tunnel with a special lady on each arm – Mrs Nessie Shankly and Mrs Jessie Paisley.

Saturday, 30 April 1994 – the last home game of the season and the emotional Kop's last stand. Raucous, witty, wise, committed, fair-minded, packed, loud and proud, and Red through and through, the Kop. If Wembley had its famous Twin Towers, Anfield had the Kop.

Merseyside icon Gerry Marsden walked towards the Kop and led the crowd in an unforgettable rendition of 'You'll Never Walk Alone' – and we all joined in. It was an occasion not to miss. And the scorer of the last goal to go into the net in front of the Kop? Jeremy Goss of Norwich City.

For the record, the unlikely scorer of Liverpool's last goal at the Kop end had come three weeks earlier when Julian Dicks converted a penalty in a 1-0 win over Ipswich Town. The scenes at the end of the Norwich City match were emotional, with many people reluctant to leave the 'spec' where they had watched the Reds over many, many years – and witnessed some extraordinary players and some extraordinary matches.

And it wasn't just the diehard Liverpool fans who revered the famous old terrace. Johan Cruyff played for Ajax in front of a full-blooded Kop at full volume in a famous European Cup tie at Anfield back in 1966: 'I really enjoyed it and Anfield was incredibly impressive. From that moment English football captured my heart.'

The actual 1993/94 season had been another turbulent one at Anfield. Graeme Souness had resigned as manager after a run of indifferent results, still, in truth, recovering and recuperating from the major operation and the dangerous after-effects that followed it. Reflecting on his spell as Liverpool manager, Souness would admit 'right man, wrong time'. A magnificent player and genuine man, he would take managerial positions across the game, and across the world. His subsequent work as a TV pundit on the game is always worthy of respect as is his charitable work. He was awarded a CBE in June 2024.

***

Local boy, born in Waterloo Hospital, Crosby in 1948, Roy Evans had been lifted off the pitch and on to the coaches' bench at the relatively tender age of 25. A former England Schoolboy international with six appearances and three goals, a 15-year-old Evans signed a 'B' form for Liverpool in January 1964. Breaking into the first team was tough for Evans, and his playing career for the Reds amounted to 11 games across five seasons. Meanwhile, he had won five reserve titles as a player between 1968 and 1974.

As reserve-team manager he would then enjoy enormous success, winning seven titles in nine years in a competition that was very important for the clubs and players competing in it. Evans was a classic 'one-club' man who took his responsibilities seriously in whatever shape and size they came. He loved the club.

Roy Evans was moved through the Boot Room ranks until, on 31 January 1994, he was appointed manager of Liverpool FC. 'Liverpool is simply the best club in the world and the fans look to the manager to provide the best for it. My aim is to restore the club to its rightful place.'

Former Liverpool player Doug Livermore was appointed as Evans's right-hand man – and a new era began at Anfield. In his first full season, 1994/95, Evans's team finished fourth in the league and enjoyed a big day out at Wembley in the Coca-Cola Cup Final on Sunday, 2 April. The Reds had beaten Burnley (over two legs), Stoke City, Blackburn Rovers, Arsenal and Crystal Palace (in a two-legged semi-final). Both games against Palace ended 1-0 – Robbie Fowler scoring a 90th-minute winner at Anfield in the first leg – and the only goal in the return leg at Selhurst Park.

Robbie Fowler became one of Liverpool's all-time greatest players. He scored goals for fun. And, most importantly, the Liverpool fans saw him as 'one of our own'. Albeit the young Fowler having been an Evertonian as a boy, with their striker Graeme Sharp being his hero. The Liverpool crowd loved him – and his team-mates did too. They knew they had a special talent in their ranks. And a real Scouser.

I saw his first-team debut at Fulham in a League Cup tie in 1993 – he scored – of course. And added all five of the goals in the return leg at Anfield! He went on to score a hat-trick in a league match with Southampton in the same month. Early in the 1994/95 season he scored a hat-trick against Arsenal at Anfield – but not just any hat-trick. He did it in double speed – three goals in the space of four minutes and 33 seconds.

Fowler, who became a close buddy of team-mate Steve McManaman, would play up front with Liverpool captain Ian Rush in the Coca-Cola Cup Final ('the League Cup Final') against First Division Bolton Wanderers. The match had greater significance because the winners would be guaranteed a place in the following season's UEFA Cup.

Roy Evans had become a great believer in playing three men at the back – the club had already invested big money in bringing Neil Ruddock to Liverpool from Spurs in 1993, and Evans added Phil Babb from Coventry City and John Scales from Wimbledon to his back line.

Liverpool's line-up for the Coca-Cola Cup Final in April 1995 looked and felt a lot different than the team that had won the FA Cup Final at Wembley in 1992. Only Rob Jones, Steve McManaman and Ian Rush featured in both teams – while goalkeeper David James, defenders Babb, Scales, Ruddock and Norwegian Stig Inge Bjørnebye joined Jones at the back, with Jamie Redknapp in midfield and Robbie Fowler up top with Rush in the Reds line-up against Bolton.

Bolton went into the final with some recent form against the Reds, having beaten them in a replayed FA Cup third-round tie in 1993 – 2-2 at Burnden Park, and a surprising 2-0 replay win for the Trotters at Anfield.

There were lots of coincidences with the Reds in the Bolton ranks. Former influential Liverpool reserve player Mark Seagraves had scored in the original third-round tie, and the Bolton captain at Wembley would be Kirkby kid Alan Stubbs, who would go on to be a great player for Everton. In midfield, Wirral-born Jason McAteer, who had played for the Republic of Ireland at the 1994 World Cup in the USA, hoped to play a big part in a Wembley victory for Bolton. His boyhood dream had been to play for Liverpool but now he was aiming to beat them underneath the Twin Towers. Game on.

* * *

It was a pleasantly warm and sunny late afternoon 5pm kick-off at Wembley Stadium as Liverpool and Bolton Wanderers vied for supremacy in a close-fought first half in front of a crowd of 75,595. Both teams had chances in the frenetic opening stages of the game. In the 37th minute, Liverpool took the lead. Steve McManaman took a pass from John Barnes and waltzed his way across the field past Alan Stubbs and then Scott Green, then placed a perfect shot past Bolton goalkeeper Keith Branagan; 1-0.

Liverpool turned the wick up in the second half and it was another beauty from Steve McManaman in the 68th minute that took them further ahead. This time, the schoolboy Everton fan, McManaman, went past Green, then McAteer, and got in front of Seagraves before once again gliding the ball into the Bolton net; 2-0.

The Lancashire side, under manager Bruce Rioch, hit back almost immediately – a defensive header from Neil Ruddock was headed back into the Liverpool area, and Bolton winger Thompson controlled the ball, swivelled and scored a fine goal. 2-1. Thompson – Alan, that is, not Peter! Although I'm sure the old Liverpool great would have loved to have seen both his Liverpool prodigy, Steve McManaman and his Bolton namesake Alan Thompson both play significant roles in the match.

Liverpool survived a late rally from Bolton to secure another trophy for the Reds. Steve McManaman proved to be the match winner and the 'Real Thing'. His outstanding performance won him the Alan Hardaker Man of the Match Award, fittingly handed over to him by the maestro, Blackpool and England winger Sir Stanley Matthews. Ian

Rush, Liverpool captain, lifted the trophy – Liverpool's fifth success in the English game's 'second' domestic cup competition.

It was a first trophy for Liverpool boss Roy Evans, qualification for the following season's UEFA Cup secured – and Bolton went on to gain promotion to the Premier League. And Jason McAteer, who had an outstanding game at Wembley in April, had his dream of playing for Liverpool fulfilled when he signed for the Anfield club in September 1995.

And Liverpool wouldn't win another piece of silverware for the rest of the decade.

***

Part Four: 'When the Cream Went Sour'

In 1975, two Italian gentlemen joined forces to create one of the most celebrated clothing brands the world has ever witnessed. Giorgio Armani and his partner, architect Sergio Galeotti, founded Giorgio Armani S.p.A, reportedly on money raised from the sale of Armani's Volkswagen. This Italian luxury fashion house, which is still based in Milan, had relatively humble beginnings but 50 years on is now a billion-dollar business with its products sold worldwide. It employs 7,000 people.

The Armani company designs, manufactures, distributes and retails haute couture, ready-to-wear leather goods, shoes and accessories, plus home interiors – and lends its name to eyewear, fragrances and cosmetics. Armani is still a hugely respected fashion group, alongside other market leaders like Gucci and Prada – and is widely regarded as a 'class act'. It is a brand that is always in the news, and whose catwalk shows are always populated by the world's most famous models as the company shows off its new designs across the world's capitals to an eager and elite clientele.

Back in 1996, one of the world's classiest fashion houses took a slight creative diversion and made headlines when they designed the 'traditional Wembley suits' for the Liverpool team, who were about to meet their arch-rivals Manchester United in that year's FA Cup Final. The suits, the accessories and the men who wore them that afternoon became as big a story as the match itself. And it is still talked about today.

Manchester United had already won their third Premier League title and were hunting down the double. Roy Evans's Liverpool had finished a respectable third in the league – and in two previous encounters with United that season had drawn 2-2 with Ferguson's men at Old Trafford before winning 2-0 at Anfield. The Old Trafford clash featured the return of United folk hero Eric Cantona, after completing his nine-month suspension following his attempted kung-fu kick at an unruly spectator at Crystal Palace.

All four Liverpool goals in those two matches were scored by Robbie Fowler, now firmly a folk hero himself to the Anfield fans – and a deadly striker who punished opponents' defensive lapses each and every time. En route to the 1996 FA Cup Final, Fowler had scored in every round of the competition: third round – Liverpool 7, Rochdale 0 (Collymore 3, Fowler, Rush, McAteer and an own goal); fourth round – Shrewsbury 0, Liverpool 4 (Collymore, Fowler, McAteer and own goal); fifth round – Liverpool 2, Charlton 1 (Fowler, Collymore); sixth round – Leeds United 0, Liverpool 0; Liverpool 3, Leeds United 0 (McManaman 2, Fowler); semi-final (at Old Trafford) Liverpool 3, Aston Villa 0 (Fowler 2, McAteer). Fowler's goals at Old Trafford in the semi-final were spectacular and set Liverpool on the way to Wembley.

An Old Trafford great, and a wonderful goalscorer himself, Scottish icon the late Denis Law praised the Liverpool striker as he previewed the forthcoming FA Cup Final:

> He reminds me of the great Jimmy Greaves at his best; over the past two years Robbie has proved that he can score goals at the very highest level, and by the time the summer comes around he could be an established international.
>
> He's like Greaves in his goalscoring in that he's deadly with anything inside the box. There are many players who when in a similar position to Robbie takes up, you don't fear any danger, but when he does that, you immediately think, 'That's going in.'

Up front with free-scoring Fowler was Liverpool's record buy, Stan Collymore, a player that on his day was unplayable – but there weren't enough of those days. He was a talented footballer whose public show of super self-confidence probably disguised a more complex personal nature.

And another player becoming a regular was goalkeeper David James. He had already tasted the sweetness of a Wembley win with Liverpool's Coca-Cola triumph against Bolton Wanderers but recognised that playing in an FA Cup Final was a step up again: 'I loved the atmosphere at Wembley, and it was a memorable day, but the FA Cup is a completely different ball game when you compare it to the League Cup. It is going to be the biggest game of my career so far. I know the fans are really up for it.'

David James was a well-honed physical specimen, and he was approached by the Italian fashion house, Armani, to do a special photoshoot for their underwear range. Whether that's the connection that got Liverpool players hooked up with Armani is unclear but what followed remains the stuff of legend. Fairly or unfairly.

The wearing of new 'clobber' on the big day at Wembley was loosely part of the tradition of the event. Invariably, it usually ended up as a smart dark-blue blazer and grey trousers, with a crisp new white shirt and club tie. So, when the Liverpool players took their pre-match stroll around a slowly filling Wembley Stadium on cup final Saturday, their choice of apparel took everybody's breath away. Cream jacket and trousers – now famously called 'white suits' – blue shirt with a blue flower in their lapel.

Accessories included Ray-Ban sunglasses and mobile phones, both of which were fully in use as the Liverpool players leisurely made their way around the pitch an hour ahead of kick-off. Of course, none of it was prejudicial to this group of talented young footballers winning the huge football match that lay ahead of them. However, you could put the argument that dressing in such a stylish but arguably 'inappropriate' fashion unhelpfully loaded unintended pressure on them.

Manager Roy Evans defended his players: 'No one would have bothered if we would have won the game.'

Sir Alex Ferguson: 'With those suits, they couldn't afford to lose. No way.'

Old Reds stalwart Ronnie Moran, who like Evans wore a more formal navy-blue attire on the day, gave a clipped, 'I'm not an ice-cream man,' when asked whether he would be wearing one of the lighter suits.

In truth, the match itself was an absolute shocker. I remember watching it in the stadium and thinking to myself, *When will somebody do something?* Anybody. In the end, and towards the end of the game, it was Manchester United's Eric Cantona who hooked home a misplaced punched ball from David James. It was a clever piece of football – and it won United the FA Cup – and the double.

And it left the Liverpool players taking a hit – style over substance – and derived from it, and other elements of some of the players' social lives and their cool acquaintances, a level of scrutiny that became intense – the moniker 'Spice Boys' was born, and it stuck. Fairly or, more likely, unfairly.

Added Time:

- On 14 February 1996, the great Bob Paisley, a wonderful servant of Liverpool Football Club, sadly passed away at the age of 77. A service of thanksgiving for his life was held a week later at his local place of worship, the Parish Church of St Peter, Woolton, where he was subsequently buried.
- Ian Rush's substitute appearance in the 1996 FA Cup Final was his final game for the club – his total of appearances for the Reds a remarkable 660 matches in which he scored 346 goals.
- Stan Collymore left Anfield after two seasons without really settling there. His total number of appearances was 81, in which he scored 35 goals.
- Euro 96 saw Anfield host three Group C games and a quarter-final in the competition – and Wembley hosted England's matches, which involved three Reds – Steve McManaman, Jamie Redknapp and Robbie Fowler.
- McManaman's performances for Terry Venables's England included a special performance in their famous 4-1 win over the Netherlands, which caught the eye of the Brazilian maestro Pelé: 'I was over in England for Euro 96 and I thought the England winger, Steve McManaman, was one of the players of the tournament.'
- The Czech Republic star, 22-year-old Patrik Berger scored a penalty in the Euro 96 Final in their 2-1 'Golden Goal' defeat to Germany at Wembley. He signed for Liverpool shortly after the tournament in August 1996 from Borussia Dortmund and made an

important contribution to the nearly 200 games he played for the Reds over the next seven years.

- And finally, in a late season Premier League match at Selhurst Park in May 1997, at the then temporary home of Wimbledon FC, a 17-year-old Liverpool player came on as a second-half substitute to make his debut for the Reds. Within minutes he had scored – and although Liverpool lost the match 2-1, the travelling supporters knew they had seen somebody and something very special. His name – Michael Owen – the rest is history.

Wembley – at last!

Just the ticket!

Billy Liddell – the ultimate 'model' footballer.

Liverpool comedy legend Ken Dodd entertains the Reds on FA Cup Final eve.

Only the ball boy separates the Liverpool and Leeds United's 'benches' – Shankly and Revie sit very close to each other and both men get absolutely soaked.

A seminal moment. The FA Cup is won and Liverpool captain, Ron Yeats, leads the celebrations.

Wembley goalscorers Ian St John and Roger Hunt immortalised.

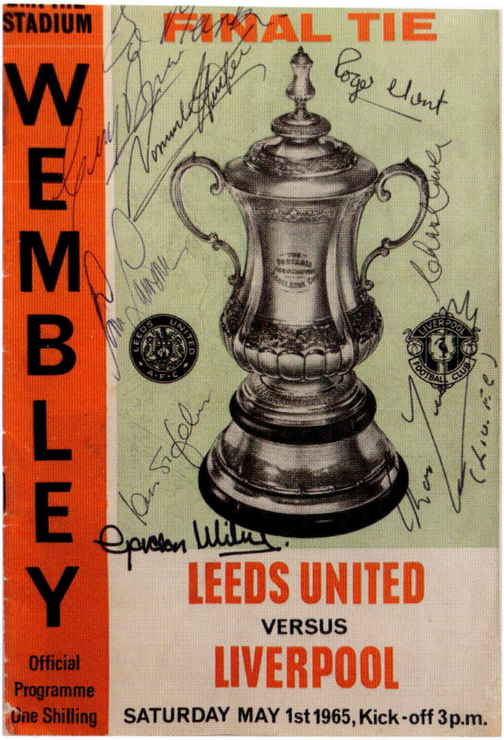

A precious memento – an FA Final programme signed by the victorious Reds.

1971 – 'Clear your throats ladies and gentlemen, it's showtime!'

Captain Emlyn Hughes and goalkeeper Ray Clemence enjoy the 1974 FA Cup Final win.

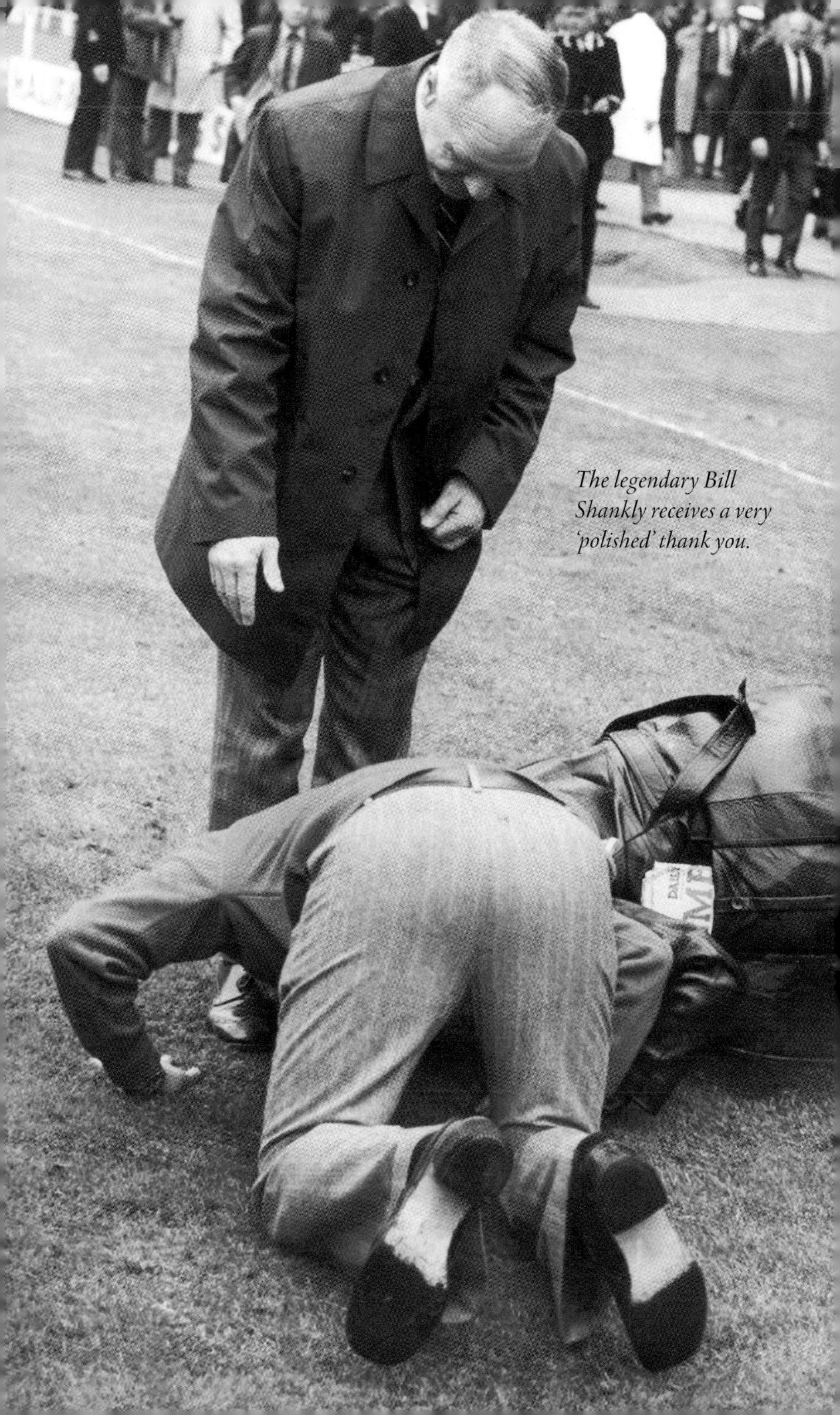

The legendary Bill Shankly receives a very 'polished' thank you.

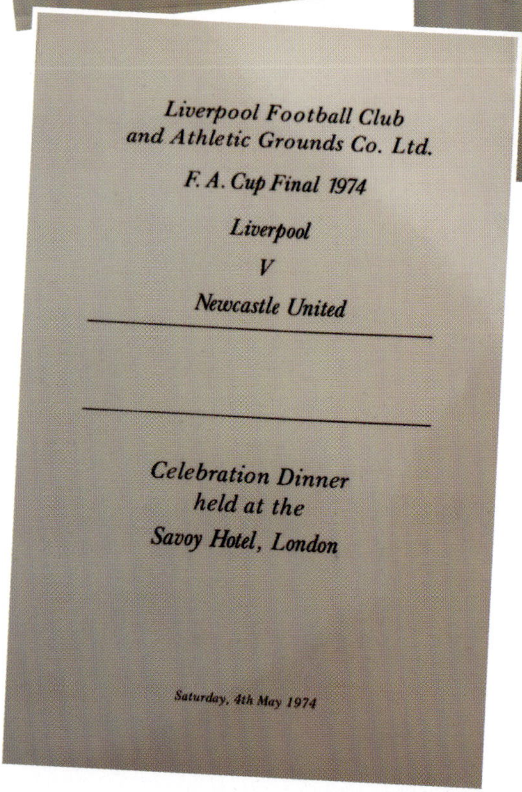

Liverpool Football Club
and Athletic Grounds Co. Ltd.

F. A. Cup Final 1974

Liverpool

V

Newcastle United

Celebration Dinner
held at the
Savoy Hotel, London

Saturday, 4th May 1974

A job well done. Now it's time to celebrate in style, and to make sure Liverpool's charismatic boss, Bill Shankly, signs your menu!

Chapter 6

The Noughties: Out with the Old, in with the New

Part One: 'Wembley Stadium Gets a Whole New Look'

One of the proudest days in my working life was on Saturday, 19 May 2007, when as CEO of the FA I had the privilege of accompanying Prince William, then President of the FA, as he walked on to the pitch at the 'new' Wembley Stadium, holding one of football's own crown jewels, the FA Cup itself, and then, with a few warm words, officially 'opened' the magnificent-looking new venue.

My long association with the famous old stadium went back to 1970, with my first visit to the ground with the Twin Towers to watch England play Northern Ireland there, before Sir Alf Ramsey's men went to Mexico and the World Cup; my first FA Cup Final there was back in 1971. And in the early 1980s my BBC duties on FA Cup Final day remarkably involved sitting cross-legged just five yards from the goal nets at the stadium's Tunnel End, ready to pick up the game's heroes for interviews when the final whistle went. I was so close to the action as to smell the players' liniment. I used to think, *And the BBC are paying me to do this!*

Before the official opening of the 'new' stadium in 2007, a parade of former FA Cup winners, including Liverpool Wembley heroes Ian St John (1965), Ray Clemence (1974),

Ian Rush (1986), John Barnes (1989) and Michael Thomas (1992), were warmly received by an excited and expectant crowd. A fly-past by the Red Arrows added to the celebratory nature of the occasion.

Ahead of us that afternoon was the 2007 FA Cup Final between Chelsea and Manchester United. And behind us years of effort, enterprise and exacting planning – and a committed desire, design and determination to make sure that in rebuilding and replacing its world-famous predecessor, justice had been done to everything that had gone before. And I might have been a bit biased – but I thought it had.

'This afternoon they are playing not just for a cup and a medal. It is sentimental and monumental,' said *The Times*.

A crowd of 89,826 witnessed Didier Drogba scoring an extra-time goal in a 1-0 win for Jose Mourinho's Chelsea men. This, on an afternoon when the world's media watched and wowed at how English football's new home looked, and a multitude of cameras, moving and still, followed every moment of the action – but as the FA's CEO, I still wanted more.

On the boardroom wall at Wembley Stadium was a famous painting by Terence Cuneo, beautifully featuring the 1962 FA Cup Final between Tottenham Hotspur and Burnley – a work of art especially commissioned to commemorate the centenary of the FA in 1963. I used to look at it every day and it gave me the idea of commissioning an artist to capture, in oils, in a triptych – a painting in three panels – another one of the FA's greatest days, the reopening of Wembley Stadium with the FA Cup Final between Chelsea and Manchester United, 19 May 2007. And that work of art still proudly hangs on the walls inside Wembley Stadium to this day.

It was a remarkable experience to see the stadium officially unveiled to the outside world – the first time with a capacity crowd. After all the hard work and heartache for the many people involved in finally getting the ambitious project over the line, it all seemed worthwhile. And while the match itself was no classic, the headlines the following day were glowing about how the stadium looked and felt.

A memorable day in the life of this particular CEO of the FA. And at the end of it I blew out a long sigh of relief … and went off and enjoyed a welcome beer or two with my mates! We were finally off and running.

***

> The new stadium is the most advanced and the best equipped in the world. However, it is also rooted in tradition, drawing on 80 years of history at Wembley to combine the spirit of the old with the best of the new.
>
> – Kenneth Powell, Architectural Historian, 2007

> The demolition of the famous Wembley twin towers just after 2pm yesterday, the final act in a long-drawn out saga, and the most significant.
>
> – Alan Pattullo, *The Scotsman*, 8 February 2003

> Wembley's arch is conceived as a triumphal gateway – a heroic symbol for the new stadium. Floodlit at night, it is a new London landmark. You can see it soaring on the skyline from the very heart of the city.
>
> Norman Foster, interviewed on BBC TV, May 2007

> I promise you, we will have an FA Cup Final there as soon as it is finished.
>
> – An exasperated Brian Barwick, CEO of the FA, any time between 2005 and 2007

The old Wembley Stadium, with its much-loved Twin Towers, stood tall as an outstanding memory of British history until it was closed in 2000, before being demolished in September 2002. The move from old to new was both a controversial and costly affair. The original stadium was loved and respected – those of us who had visited it cherished the memory of a great game, a great goal or just a great time we had enjoyed there.

However, the stadium had become a little dilapidated, and, in truth, was becoming no longer fit for purpose. It was the right time to move on. One personal example was the famous time-served rickety old lift that took all the TV and radio presenters, commentators, pundits, cameramen and engineers up to their working positions on the morning of the big sporting occasions.

We would all queue up nervously before, a few at a time, being crammed into a small space as the lift, manned by a bloke as old as the lift itself, slowly rattled itself up to the commentary and camera positions, high in the stadium roof, with everybody crossing their fingers until it finally landed at the TV balcony and abruptly stopped with a sudden jolt. And then everybody subsequently spent the rest of the afternoon crossing their legs once there – there were no loos on that level!

When I joined the FA as the organisation's CEO back in January 2005, I spent my second day in the job going over to Wembley Stadium from our base in Soho Square. Hard hat on, and safety lecture digested, I went around the building site that had been the old Wembley and now was being reconstructed into the new Wembley. I'm no expert, but I knew just being led around the site that there was plenty of work still to be done – and any deadline that was supposed to see the project completed was very unlikely to be met. Or price for its completion.

Indeed, one of the things I did, in due course, was to book the Millennium Stadium for the 2006 FA Cup Final – some considerable time before some of the so-called experts on the Wembley Stadium board told me I needed to. On this occasion, my caution paid off as, when the 2006 FA Cup Final between Liverpool and West Ham United kicked off in Cardiff, there were still thousands of seats still to be installed back at Wembley.

The design of the new stadium was seen as both functional and architecturally significant. Sir Norman Foster designed the arch and the roof structure. The Arch has a real job to do – it supports the roof structure, which means every one of the 90,000 stadium seats has an unobstructed view of the pitch – but it also provides a remarkable image when lit up before a match or to celebrate in the colours of a winning team.

Some other numbers: the stadium encloses four million cubic metres within the walls and under the roof. The stadium roof rises 52 metres above the pitch, and the circumference of the building is one kilometre. The seating is much more steeply banked than previously so that no seat has a restricted view, and the seats have more legroom. The stadium has 26 lifts, 30 sets of escalators, 164 turnstiles, 34 bars, eight restaurants, and 688 food and drink kiosks … and 2,618 toilets!

To overcome financial concerns over the building of the new stadium, the parties involved came to an agreement on a fixed-cost contract. This made provision for a building cost of around £352 million, with total project costs of £757 million. The final stadium costs finally came in at around £800 million.

Some people have grown to love the 'new' stadium, while some people think it lacks the atmosphere of its older version. What hasn't changed is the name. 'Wembley' remains synonymous with big football occasions of domestic, European and world sporting status – massive contemporary open-air concerts from the iconic Live Aid in 1985 to eight sold-out nights of American musical phenomenon, Taylor Swift, in 2024, the London concerts for the return of Oasis in 2025, and for hosting other sports showpiece events, from world championship boxing, Rugby League Challenge Cup finals and NFL sell-outs to the football tournament in the 2012 Olympic Games.

The new stadium had to get over a few early gremlins, as could be expected, including getting the famous pitch properly bedded down and 100 per cent fit for the purpose of elite sport. In the years that have followed, the stadium has shown its remarkable flexibility. No more so than the following double-header …

On Friday evening, 30 May 2014, England beat Peru 3-0 in an international friendly attended by 87,578 football fans. Overnight, the stadium was reconfigured, including putting seating across a covered pitch and the constructing of a boxing ring(!) around the centre circle, to host the much-anticipated rematch between world super-middleweight champion Carl Froch and his British arch-rival, George Groves, on the night of 31 May 2014, in front of a crowd of 80,000. I went to both events and couldn't get over how smooth the transition from hosting one type of sport to another had been.

As the years pass, the 'new' Wembley will create its own bank of memories for future generations who will still cherish their day at the national stadium and the special moments that it so often delivers.

* * *

Dietmar Hamann was a German footballer who played for Wacker Munich, Bayern Munich, Newcastle United, Liverpool, Manchester City and MK Dons. He was a clever midfield player who was a serial trophy winner for Bayern Munich and Liverpool. He also won 59 caps for Germany – and won a runners-up medal in the 2002 World Cup against Brazil. He was also the player who scored the last goal at the original Wembley Stadium – a feat still remembered to this day.

A rainy, miserable afternoon – 7 October 2000 – was the day England and Germany met at Wembley Stadium in a World Cup qualifying group game. We were all there to watch what was normally a close tussle between two great footballing rivals, and to reminisce about all the many times we had been to matches (and world title fights and concerts, etc.) in the world's most famous stadium, fully understanding that this was a poignant yet definitive moment in English sporting history. The England boss, former Liverpool legend Kevin Keegan, had called for his players to produce a memorable performance to mark the occasion.

Instead, it was Liverpool midfielder Dietmar Hamann, born in Waldsassen in 1973, who added a final memory – and a tough one to take for the home fans. Hamann: 'After 13 minutes we got a free kick a long way out. I thought in the difficult conditions if I could hit it quick it might just catch England out.' And it did.

Hamann's goal turned out to be the only goal of the game – a winning goal for Germany, and the chorus of booing at the end of the game must have been an added ingredient to why Kevin Keegan resigned as England manager immediately after the game. It was not the way it should have all ended.

An amusing postscript to Hamann's goal was when the London Development Agency was looking for a name for its bridge into the new stadium. Mischievous online support for it to be named the 'Hamann Bridge' sprung out of Germany and was endorsed by those with traditional sporting rivalries with England – there were quite a few! Despite the 'Hamann

Bridge' being a clear winner, the Agency declared it 'offside' and the bridge was ultimately named White Horse Bridge in honour of Billy, the famous police horse that helped control the crowds at the inaugural Wembley FA Cup Final in 1923.

Added Time:

- In September 2001, England gained revenge over Germany with a stunning 5-1 win in their return World Cup qualifier in Munich. All the goals were scored by Liverpool players – Michael Owen scoring a hat-trick, Steven Gerrard and Emile Heskey adding the others. The Reds' Nick Barmby and substitute Jamie Carragher also played their part.
- The illuminated scoreboard with its Deutschland/England 1:5 remains a lasting image of a very special night.

***

Part Two: 'Croeso I Gaerdydd' – 'And Welcome to Anfield South … Wales!'

As the planet entered its third millennium, it is worth briefly pausing to explore the origins of the sport we all love – and one that continues to sweep the world – across its many continents, countries and cities, including a football-mad place we all love called Liverpool.

The game has become an absolute obsession to its legion of followers – generation after generation after generation. And, in turn, football has become a super-rich trillion-dollar business while still retaining its eternal appeal as a wonderful form of social and physical exercise for all the rest of us mere mortals.

FIFA officially acknowledge that during the Han Dynasty in China (206 BC–AD 220) a game called Cuju or 'kickball' could claim to be the very earliest form of the sport.

The first unambiguous reference to football in England is a writ for preserving the peace in London, dated 13 April 1314, which notes 'the great uproar in the city, through certain tumults arising from the striking of large footballs in the public fields'.

In 1605, the great bard himself, William Shakespeare, reflected an association with a sport he's thought to have played in his classic tragedy *King Lear*, when Kent taunted Oswald, 'Nor tripped, neither you base-football player.' The first mention of the very modern act of simulation!?

And, in one of Shakespeare's earlier works, *The Comedy of Errors*, Dromio asked Adriana, 'Am I so round with you as you with me, that like a football do you spurn me thus.' The play's title is a much-used cliché employed by commentators and writers to this day, when a series of self-inflicted mistakes between team-mates ends in a disaster for those involved.

That other perennial post-match classic, 'over the moon', would seem to have emanated from a 1718 work, *The Coquet*, by Charles Molloy. And the opening lines of Charles Dickens's much admired *A Tale of Two Cities* has given members of the football family a short sentence to capture all possible likelihoods in a long, hard season: 'It was the best of times; it was the worst of times.'

***

As the Liverpool players entered the new millennium, they were now under the leadership of Frenchman Gérard Houllier, who, with his professorial manner, found his own lyrical galactic prose to set new sky-high targets for his Anfield men: 'Aim for the moon and maybe you land in the stars.'

And, in due course, Liverpool Football Club's very own French romantic, Houllier, could look back with some satisfaction after the Reds had a real lift-off with three trophies inside 90 days, and reached an invaluably high position in the Premier League in what became a bloated 63-game, but ultimately triumphant, 2000/01 season for the Anfield men.

Those trophies were fittingly won in the Millennium Stadium. In Cardiff. A brand-new stadium. The venue, now called the Principality Stadium, opened in 1999 to host that year's Rugby World Cup, and with its nearly 74,000 capacity and a roof that would close, it housed many of the big domestic football occasions for several early years of the new decade while the natural home for those matches, Wembley, was being rebuilt and reshaped.

And, for Liverpool fans, Liverpool to Cardiff became a regular trip to make – a few miles shorter than a journey to Wembley, and to a stadium conveniently built in the very heart of the Welsh capital. And the Reds played there in trophy-hunting matches eight times in six years.

'Anfield South' quickly became 'Anfield South Wales'.

***

Part Three: 'The Memorable Millennium Matches'

Sunday, 25 February 2001 – the Worthington Cup Final

After five seasons without any silverware, Liverpool were finally able to unlock their trophy cabinet with a dramatic penalty shoot-out win over Birmingham City in Cardiff. Robbie Fowler, captaining the side in the Worthington Cup Final – essentially the Football League Cup Final – put Liverpool ahead in the 30th minute with a left-foot rocket. It was a belter, even by Fowler's high standards.

Fowler's wonderful goal looked certain to be the winner until, in stoppage time, Liverpool defender Stéphane

Henchoz gave away a penalty with a reckless challenge and Birmingham's Darren Purse duly dispatched the spot kick. Extra time – Liverpool, and Henchoz, survived another careless tackle, and Fowler had a brilliant header saved, so the game went to a penalty shoot-out.

At 4-4 in the shoot-out, with both teams having missed one, it went to sudden death. Up stepped Jamie Carragher, who safely dispatched his 12-yarder, then Birmingham's Andy Johnson was the unfortunate fall guy who missed his. Liverpool had won the League Cup for the sixth time, and Robbie Fowler, who had scored the first-half scorcher and the Reds' fifth penalty in the shoot-out, collected the cup, plus the Alan Hardaker Trophy as man of the match.

The Reds were off and running in a remarkable sequence of trophy-lifting that would tally five by the end of the summer.

Saturday, 12 May 2001 – the FA Cup Final

Three things stand out for me about the 2001 FA Cup Final. Firstly, it was a boiling-hot day in the Welsh sunshine – boiling. Secondly, how Liverpool won the match is a complete mystery; opponents Arsenal could and should have won it three or four times over. And thirdly, those present at the Millennium Stadium that afternoon were privileged to witness a single individual turn a football match on its head – and guarantee that the 2001 FA Cup Final would be forever remembered in his name. And he lived in Wales.

Firstly, let's deal with the heat. I've watched football in the many vagaries of the wonderfully unpredictable British weather. I've been frozen, soaked, windswept and, on one occasion, snowed on while sitting *inside* the main stand at Newcastle, and, of course, like other folk, been caught out many a time wearing the wrong gear on the wrong day. But that afternoon in May in Cardiff was, by some distance, the hottest I've ever been while watching a football match.

Representing ITV Sport in the VIP seats in the Millennium Stadium, I settled into the occasion only to quickly realise we were in the direct line of the hot afternoon sun – and with no cover. By half-time I looked decidedly red – RED – and, frankly, had noticed people pointing me out to their colleagues. At this point, a very kind lady approached me and said: 'I've been watching you getting redder and redder as the first half went on – and I've got three things for you – here's a bottle of ice-cold water, a small tube of suntan lotion and a baseball cap that I found under my seat. Please have them.'

I can't remember what the cap was advertising, but on to my head it went. I then slapped a generous amount of 'Factor 30' on my face and with a cold drink in my hand went back to my seat for the second half – and watched football history being made.

It was the first FA Cup Final where the managers were from outside of the British Isles – Gérard Houllier and Arsène Wenger driving a French revolution through the game. Their tactics may have differed but their theories on player preparation, diet and social behaviour matched up – and each set high standards for their group, which meant, in due course, some players fell by their respective waysides.

The North London club should have enjoyed their third FA Cup win over Liverpool but couldn't get the vital goal despite having chance after chance. And when they eventually did get ahead through a Freddie Ljungberg goal in the 72nd minute, they couldn't add a decisive second. A worldwide TV audience of over 600 million were absorbed by the game – and just 11 minutes after Ljungberg's strike, the Reds were level – and then ahead.

The young man who turned the 2001 FA Cup Final on its head was Chester-born Michael Owen, who lived with his family in North Wales. He had already earned legendary status with his remarkable goal for England against Argentina in the 1998 World Cup in France. His two-goal burst inside five minutes in the Millennium Stadium also secured his place in FA Cup Final history – and his name became instantly synonymous with that game.

Michael Owen had the ultimate day to remember. He had originally meant to wear a new pair of boots for the big match, but when Phil Thompson and Gérard Houllier heard of it, they persuaded him against doing so. Whether it was a bit of suspicion or not, Owen stuck with his old Umbro favourites.

'Once we had equalised [83 mins], I was certain we would win. As soon as I scored my first, I knew we would win ...'

His second goal in the 88th minute was a classic. Patrik Berger played a long ball upfield. Owen sprinted past Lee Dixon and took the ball to the side of Tony Adams, who was racing to intercept. Too late. Owen had the run on the Arsenal defender and then his precisely placed shot went past David Seaman's diving hand into the Gunners' goal. The Liverpool fans behind the Arsenal goal went absolutely crazy – and why not!

And Michael Owen celebrated his winning goal with a now-famous somersault. And why not! He had just almost single-handedly won the FA Cup for Liverpool – against the run of play, against the odds and against the club that had beaten them in the 1950 and 1971 FA Cup finals.

The 'Michael Owen Final' was born and lives on alongside the likes of the 1953 'Matthews Final', and will forever and a day. The Englishman, who lived in Wales, had delivered the decisive coup de grâce for his French boss, Monsieur Houllier. As he often did, Houllier had a literary take on the famous 'Victoire Palpitant': 'On some occasions the will to win is more important than the skill to win.'

The following midweek, Liverpool would win a remarkable UEFA Cup Final against Spanish side Alavés, 5-4 in Germany – via one of their opponents, Geli, scoring an own goal in a match that was settled in extra time by the scoring of a 'golden goal'. And, seven days after celebrating an FA Cup Final in Cardiff, a 4-0 win in South East London against Charlton Athletic secured a place in the following season's UEFA Champions League. C'est magnifique!

Sunday, 12 August 2001 – the FA Charity Shield

The first time that the traditional curtain-raiser to the football season was played in Cardiff was also the last time the match would be played under the title of the FA Charity Shield, first given it in 1908. The 79th Charity Shield match featured Liverpool, the FA Cup winners, and Manchester United, the 2000/01 Premier League champions, watched by a crowd of 70,227 at the Millennium Stadium.

And, although seen by many as an event in which the result didn't matter as much as the outcomes of those many matches that lay ahead of them in the long season to follow, a tussle between the two footballing giants of the North West of England guaranteed fireworks – from the start!

Liverpool opened the scoring in the second minute of the match when Gary McAllister scored from the penalty spot after Roy Keane had fouled Danny Murphy. Michael Owen (who else!) put Liverpool further ahead in the 16th minute, and despite Ruud van Nistelrooy pulling one back early in the second half, Alex Ferguson's men couldn't turn the game around. Trophy number four for Liverpool – despite being without two of their home-grown stars, Steven Gerrard, out injured, and Robbie Fowler, left out of the matchday squad as his fall-out with the Reds' assistant manager, Phil Thompson, following a training ground incident, rumbled on. Thompson said a ball fired at full pelt towards him and that had hit him on the head was deliberate – Fowler, who struck the ball, said it wasn't. The two men still hadn't settled their differences.

Twelve days later, Liverpool would pick up their fifth trophy of the year, beating European champions Bayern Munich in the UEFA Super Cup, held in the Stade Louis II in Monaco. The Reds had led 3-0, with goals from John Arne Riise, Emile Heskey and Michael Owen, before the Germans pulled two goals back to make the closing stages of the game tense for the Anfield men. But they got there in the end. Michael Owen won the man of the match award – and later would win the prized Ballon d'Or.

Added Time:

- As I settled into my seat on a train taking me from Euston Station to Liverpool's UEFA Champions League opening group game against Boavista of Portugal, a member of the train staff who I knew said, 'Hey, Brian, have you heard what is happening in New York and across the States?' I hadn't – but quickly got up to speed on the extraordinary matters taking place across the Atlantic. It was an unprecedented terrorist attack on the USA, on the World Trade Center, with the barely believable collapsing of the Twin Towers in New York and a full-scale attack on other strategic targets in the USA. Thousands of people died in a dreadful terrorist atrocity; 11 September 2001; '9/11'.
- In October, Liverpool manager Gérard Houllier was taken ill and didn't emerge from the dressing room area at the end of the half-time break in a match between Liverpool and Leeds United at Anfield.

Houllier was rushed to Broadgreen Hospital, where he underwent immediate life-saving surgery that lasted several hours. He had an acute dissection of his aorta repaired. It had been touch-and-go.

- As the Frenchman underwent a long period of rest and recuperation, Phil Thompson picked up the managerial reins, calmed down his emotional touchline style and did very well deputising for his friend and colleague, Gérard Houllier.
- An uncomfortable truce broke out between Thompson and Fowler over the training ground incident but in November, Liverpool's brilliant striker, the fans' favourite, left Anfield to join Leeds United. He would return to his spiritual home at a later date.

Sunday, 11 August 2002 – the FA Community Shield

After three successful outings to the Millennium Stadium, Liverpool had settled into the groove on their Welsh days out. Birmingham City, Arsenal and Manchester United had been put to the sword – and next up in the newly named, and framed, FA Community Shield, the Gunners would again be the opposition for Houllier's men. The renaming of the competition was to better reflect how the monies raised would be distributed – and with a swanky new sponsor of 'Presenting Partner' in the burger giant of giants, McDonald's, who had gone the whole hog themselves employing England hero Sir Geoff Hurst as its Director of Football.

Arsenal arrived at the Millennium Stadium as both Premier League champions and FA Cup winners, their 2-0 win over Chelsea in the final helping them to the double. They had knocked out Liverpool en route to the final. By finishing runners-up in the Premier League, albeit seven points adrift of Arsène Wenger's men, Liverpool had been invited to play in yet another Charity Shield/Community Shield curtain-raiser.

The game itself was won by a single goal by Arsenal's Gilberto Silva. A small consolation following their traumatic experience at the hands of the Reds in 2001. It is not known whether Arsène Wenger celebrated the win with a quarter pounder and an appropriately named portion of French fries!

Sunday, 2 March 2003 – the Worthington Cup Final

Liverpool manage Gérard Houllier had done his 'shopping' before the start of the 2002 World Cup in Japan and South Korea. He had released Nicolas Anelka after his short loan spell at Anfield from Paris Saint-Germain – a move that surprised some of his Liverpool team-mates, who had found the Frenchman to be far more fun than that of his image as something of a sulky character.

Meanwhile, Houllier, an ever-present at UEFA and FIFA events, had been persuaded to aid his recovery from his major surgery and watch the tournament on TV from the comfort of his favourite armchair at his home.

In what seemed a classic 'under the radar' transfer coup, Houllier bought two stars of the Senegal team that would do well in the World Cup. Striker El Hadji Diouf and midfielder Salif Diao were signed from French clubs, Lens and Sedan respectively. Indeed, Diouf signed his contract on the morning of the opening game of the 2002 World Cup between holders France, and Senegal. And the African Player of the Year starred in his country's surprise win over a French team that would ultimately take an early plane home from the tournament. Salif Diao scored one of the goals of the tournament against Denmark – and then got sent off in the same game.

A third new face at Anfield would be the 24-year-old midfielder Bruno Cheyrou. Rather grandly described by Houllier as 'the next Zidane', Cheyrou was signed from Lille. His promise was never fully realised (unless Houllier was talking about 'another Zidane'!). Indeed, all three of those purchases, amounting to about £20m, failed to live up to their expectations. Within weeks of arriving at Melwood, the Reds' famous training ground, Diouf was already the 'last pick' when the end-of-session five-a-side teams were chosen by his team-mates.

Liverpool's 2002/03 Premier League season started remarkably well – nine wins and three draws in the opening 12 games, followed by an extraordinary run of the next 11 games without a win – six defeats and five draws. The Reds would ultimately finish in fifth position in the Premier League, out of the Champions League slots. They had also gone out of that season's Champions League competition itself at the group stage and exited the FA Cup in the fourth round.

It was only in the League Cup that the Reds excelled. In the Worthington Cup they beat Southampton and Ipswich Town, followed up by an exciting 4-3 away victory over Aston Villa. Sheffield United were dispatched in the two-legged semi-final, setting up another trip to Cardiff for Reds supporters – and another match against arch-rivals Manchester United.

In goal for the Reds that day was a Polish keeper, Jerzy Dudek. He had been signed by Liverpool on the same day as they bought another goalkeeper, Chris Kirkland. The latter would be plagued by injuries throughout his time with the Reds, whereas Dudek was on a footballing journey that would ultimately make him a legend at Anfield. Signed from Feyenoord on 31 August 2001, Dudek would go on to make 186 appearances for Liverpool in his six seasons at Anfield.

After an outstanding first season between the sticks, a horror show against Manchester United on 1 December 2002, when he famously gift-wrapped two goals for Diego Forlan, led to him being replaced by Kirkland.

But Chris Kirkland's injury frailty let Dudek back in the team in late January 2003 – and a place in the team chosen to meet Manchester United in the Worthington Cup Final in Cardiff in March of that year.

And as so often happens in football, from being the fall guy in the pre-Christmas game against United, Dudek was Liverpool's hero against the same opposition when the two teams met at the Millennium Stadium. This time for a trophy. Liverpool went ahead through a brilliant 39th-minute goal from Steven Gerrard, which took a deflection from David Beckham, and past Fabien Barthez in the Manchester United goal. The result was wrapped up in the 86th minute by a 'clincher' from the goal machine, Michael Owen.

Between Gerrard's and Owen's goals, Jerzy Dudek pulled off save after save to thwart the Manchester United forwards. He was simply superb. Post-match, Gérard Houllier said, 'I told Jerzy three days ago, I can feel you will be the hero. You were unlucky when we played them late last year, today you were the man of the match.'

Post-match, Sir Alex Ferguson: 'Dudek won them the cup.'

Dudek himself was a modest soul, who took the ups and downs of being a goalkeeper in his stride. And two years later he would earn his legendary status with a very special save in the 'Miracle in Istanbul'. When he finished his football career, he turned to motorsport to get his competitive kicks. He raced high-speed sports cars in top-class events around Europe, including a stint behind the steering wheel in the world-famous Le Mans 24-hour race. Well, they do say all goalkeepers are crazy!!

Sunday, 27 February 2005 – the Carling Cup Final

The summer of 2004 marked two significant cultural newcomers to British family life. On 15 May 2004, a TV programme that would become a surefire Saturday night treat began its life. *Strictly Come Dancing* hit the BBC screens in an early summer-time try-out, and such was its success that its next series the following year saw it moved into the autumn and it has been a peak-time hit for the BBC for the past 20 years.

With compere Bruce Forsyth at its helm, a group of judges headed by the loveable and experienced Len 'well, you could pickle my walnuts' Goodman, and a mix of brilliant professional dancers and celebrity beginners, the early series caught the imagination of the British public. The winners of the first series? Newsreader Natasha Kaplinsky and professional 'hoofer' Brendan Cole.

Another new show launched that year to less public acclaim has proved a saviour for many parents of toddlers. *Peppa Pig*, a cartoon for under-fives, has calmed the storm in many a young household. It began its life on Channel 5 in 2004 and has become a smash hit the world over, as 180 countries now follow the exploits of Peppa and her pig family and animal friends. And, as grandparents, my wife and I can confirm that Peppa has often proved a winner in quelling a 'local and temporary' storm!

In football, the summer of 2004, England went out of the Euros after a quarter-final penalty shoot-out against hosts Portugal. Surprise packet Greece were the eventual winners of the competition. And two Premier League clubs chasing down the Arsenal team of 'Invincibles', who had won the previous season's title without losing a game, made big changes. Liverpool appointed the coach of Valencia, Rafa Benítez, as their new man. The first Spanish manager in

English football, Benítez had two La Liga titles under his belt and a UEFA Cup win over Marseilles. He would play a huge role in resetting the dial for the Reds.

A Liverpool player going in the opposition direction was Michael Owen, who left to join his England team-mate David Beckham at Real Madrid. Chelsea, benefitting from the riches of their new owner, Russian Roman Abramovich, signed up UEFA Champions League winners Porto's coach, Jose Mourinho. Mourinho, who had been an assistant coach under Bobby Robson at Barcelona, would prove to be a huge hit at Stamford Bridge. He gave himself the rather grandiose title of the 'Special One' – and the media gobbled up his every word from thereon in.

Between October 2004 and August 2007, Liverpool's Benítez and Chelsea's Mourinho would lock horns no less than 16 times across five competitions – the Premier League, the UEFA Champions League, the FA Cup, the Football League Cup and the Community Shield. It became an absorbing rivalry between the two clubs and the two top-flight managers.

* * *

The year of 2004 was an important one on a personal level. After 25 years at the sharp end of TV sports broadcasting – 18 years at BBC Sport and seven at ITV Sport – working on all the major global and domestic sporting events, the channels' most iconic programme titles, and with some of the country's most talented presenters, commentators and pundits – having given many of them their first job in the industry – it was time to move on.

A vacancy at the FA came up, and, given my love of the sport, my extensive knowledge of its history and heritage, and my network of key 'players' in it, I felt it was worth throwing my hat in the ring and applied for the job as Chief Executive

Officer of the oldest governing body in world football. And after two interviews, and it would seem seeing off the competition of some 400 other applicants, I got the job.

That was in November 2004, and I began in my new role in January 2005. It was something of a seismic change, but I threw myself into it – and for the best part of four years saw the sport from every angle, had some fantastic days and some really tough ones too. That was the job.

It was also the reason I was in Cardiff in February 2005, representing, with others, the FA at the annual meeting of the International Football Association Board (IFAB).

Historically, this board was made up of the four domestic governing bodies – England, Scotland, Northern Ireland and Wales – and FIFA, with President Sepp Blatter and Michel Platini among others in attendance, reflecting the will of the rest of the global football family.

It was a forum that carried significant weight, not least discussing and deliberating on changes in the laws of the game – or introducing other nuances to bring the sport into line with developments in other major sports. The voting structure gave each of the domestic bodies one vote apiece, FIFA had four votes, and for any decision to be passed, six votes were needed. In essence, the weight of vote sat with FIFA.

I kept quiet during my experience of an IFAB meeting, being held in Wales, but for the next three years made a strong case for GLT – goal-line technology – understanding how it would work, that it would deal with a matter of fact; that is, the whole of the ball had to be over the whole of the line, and critically, that it was instantaneous. I never got its use passed in my time in the FA job, but it eventually got across the line, so to speak! I think Frank Lampard's 'goal that was never given' in England's high-profile match against Germany in the 2010 World Cup was the moment opinions changed.

As part of the IFAB weekend, which went to different countries in turn, the members would go to see a match together. The IFAB meeting in 2005 in Wales coincided with the staging of the Football League Cup Final so we all went off to the Millennium Stadium to see the Carling Cup Final between Liverpool and Chelsea.

Mourinho and Benítez were making their mark, and in the two Premier League matches between the two sides the Londoners had the edge – two 1-0 wins, with Joe Cole scoring the winner in each game. He would later have a short spell at Anfield too.

The two teams lined up for the first domestic trophy of the season in front of a crowd of nearly 72,000 fans, each coach having taken the competition reasonably lightly until it got to the sharp end. But these two guys were used to winning trophies, and an intriguing climax to this season's Football League Cup – the Carling Cup – was in store.

* * *

Liverpool scored in the first minute of the game – the fastest goal ever scored in the final of this competition. The Reds' Fernando Morientes ran over to the right-hand side of the pitch, and his cross to the edge of the Chelsea penalty area was met by midfielder John Arne Riise, who volleyed the ball past Petr Čech into the Londoners' net. It was a stunning goal.

It was late in the game, the 79th minute, when Steven Gerrard, seemingly a Mourinho transfer target, unfortunately diverted a Chelsea free kick into his own net to level the score. Chelsea manager Jose Mourinho's subsequent touchline antics, putting his finger to his lips in front of the Liverpool fans, got him sent to the stands. He later suggested his gesture was aimed at the media not the fans.

The match went into extra time and, in its second half, Drogba and Kežman gave Chelsea a two-goal advantage.

A goal for Liverpool from substitute Antonio Nuñez wasn't enough to help pull the Reds back into the match – and Mourinho had won his first trophy with Chelsea.

But the Liverpool and Chelsea business for the season wasn't done yet. And some. The clubs would meet again in the two-legged semi-final of that season's UEFA Champions League. The first leg at Stamford Bridge ended goalless. The second leg in front of an Anfield crowd that was absolutely buzzing was won by a single goal scored early in the match by Liverpool's Spanish winger, Luis Garcia.

Chelsea players were convinced his effort hadn't crossed the goal line – and Mourinho felt the phenomenal atmosphere in the stadium was influential in the referee and his assistants letting the goal stand.

It was the game's only goal. Liverpool, of course, would go on to have a 'Miracle Night in Istanbul' and Chelsea would win the Premier League title, their first championship success since 1955.

Saturday, 13 May 2006 – the FA Cup Final

The 2006 FA Cup Final between Liverpool and West Ham United climaxed the 125th season of world football's oldest knockout competition. That made it special – but so did the match itself. An absolute cracker with some special goals and the drama of a penalty shoot-out to decide the fate of the two finalists.

Liverpool had beaten Luton Town 5-3 in the FA Cup third round after trailing 3-1 at one point. Portsmouth were put to the sword 2-1 in the fourth round, then a Peter Crouch goal clinched a 1-0 home win against Manchester United in the fifth round. Birmingham City were destroyed 7-0 at the Midlanders' own ground in the sixth round, the Reds biggest-ever away win in the FA Cup.

The Reds' semi-final at Old Trafford pitched them against their new hottest rivals, Chelsea, and this time the Reds came out of another tight tussle as 2-1 winners. In the 2006 FA Cup Final match programme, Rafa Benítez set out his views ahead of the big game:

> At every level of this club we want to win every match we play in and every cup we compete for. If we lift the FA Cup today, it will complete a unique double for us. Last month, our under-18s won the FA Youth Cup, which was a great achievement. Now, it's really important for the players to win the cup.

Rafa Benítez's FA Cup Final starting line-up read thus: Reina; Finnan, Carragher, Hyypiä, Riise; Sissoko, Alonso, Gerrard, Kewell; Crouch, Cissé. Substitutes, all used, were Morientes, Hamann and Kromkamp.

The 2006 FA Cup Final was the last staged in Cardiff before the competition's climax returned to its spiritual home at Wembley – the 'new' Wembley Stadium. It also proved to be one of my own 'special days'. The appointment of Prince William as new President of the FA had been seen as a positive move, and the 2006 FA Cup Final was to be his first public outing in the role. As the kick-off approached, I took him down in the lift into the bowels of the Millennium Stadium, where we stood at the back of the tunnel and watched as the two teams emerged from their respective dressing rooms.

Prince William briefly exchanged glances with Steven Gerrard, who broke into a broad smile, shyly returned by our royal guest. The pre-match ritual of 'meeting the teams' – as the day's chief guest is introduced to the players – duly followed. On this occasion, I was in the presentation party with our new president, now the Prince of Wales, and Patron of the FA.

It momentarily took me back to 1965, and watching, with my family, on our black-and-white TV set as Prince Philip, the Duke of Edinburgh, was introduced to the Liverpool and Leeds United teams that afternoon. Now 41 years later I was accompanying his grandson on the same traditional pre-match protocol, before settling back to watch 'my' team play in the FA Cup Final. As I made my way along the West Ham players, I made it my business to be strenuously fair-minded, but I'm sure there was just a little bit of extra oomph in my handshakes with the Liverpool team.

Anyway, to the TV viewers, any illusions of neutrality went out of the window when the BBC commentator, my old mate, the late John Motson, said, 'Brian Barwick there, a staunch Liverpudlian who has supported the team all his life.' Thanks Motty!

The match itself was a belter. The Hammers went 1-0 up through a Jamie Carragher own goal, and Dean Ashton added a close-range second for the London side. Four minutes later Gerrard played a perfect ball through to Cissé, who finished with typical French flair. Into the second half, and Gerrard, who else, pulled the Reds level 2-2. But West Ham weren't done, and full-back Paul Konchesky lofted a cross into the Reds' box, which Pepe Reina misread; 3-2 to West Ham.

I had made sure that my FA colleague, and Hammers legend, Trevor Brooking was sitting near me, and Prince William enjoyed watching our constrained joy or despair as either of our teams scored or conceded a goal.

The match was in injury time, and the FA Cup was heading off to the East End of London, when Steven Gerrard pulled it out of the fire for Liverpool – once again – scoring a goal voted in a BBC viewers' poll back in 2015 as the greatest goal scored in the FA Cup Final from the previous 50 years. Whatever, it was a goal that stunned both Reds and

Hammers fans and his 35-yard last-gasp screamer took the game into extra time. No more goals were scored.

Liverpool went on to win the cup on penalties, Reina saving three West Ham spot kicks. And Prince William handed the priceless piece of sporting silverware to Steven Gerrard. The 'Gerrard Final' was complete.

Sunday, 13 August 2006 – the FA Community Shield

This was FA Cup winners Liverpool's 21st appearance in the season's traditional curtain-raiser, and for their opponents, Premier League champions Chelsea, it was their sixth time. And it was the 11th time the two sides had met since the start of the 2004/05 season. They would play each other four more times before the end of the upcoming 2006/07 season, including another two-legged UEFA Champions League semi-final. Remarkable in many ways.

For the Community Shield match, Liverpool started with Steven Gerrard and Xabi Alonso on the bench, as Benítez tried to match up levels of fitness alongside trying to win the trophy. They would join the action an hour into the game. Alonso was booked within a minute! Liverpool had gone ahead in the ninth minute of the match through John Arne Riise, a player increasingly the scorer of important and, invariably, dramatic goals.

Jose Mourinho had brought AC Milan's Andriy Shevchenko to Chelsea, and he was on hand to level the scores just before half-time. The winning goal came in the 80th minute with Peter Crouch heading home to add another entry on to the Liverpool's honours list.

Crouch post-match: 'There's a bit of rivalry between the two sides and it is great to get an early one over them. Make no mistake, this is a big game to win and could give us the psychological edge over them.'

With Wembley Stadium now looking extremely likely to be finished before the end of the 2006/07 season – it was – the FA Community Shield match would prove to be the final game played at the Millennium Stadium by Liverpool.

It had been an exciting set of eight matches, in which six of them were won by the Reds – and three different domestic trophies lifted – the FA Cup twice, the Football League Cup twice and the FA Charity/Community Shield twice. They had enjoyed their time in South Wales and their next target would be to get to play at the new Wembley Stadium.

Surprisingly, it would take over five years to reach the new Wembley. Meanwhile, it was thank you and goodbye to Cardiff, the Millennium Stadium … and 'Anfield South … Wales'!

Chapter 7

The 2010s: Back in the Old Routine

Part One: The Long Wait Is Over … Nearly!

When the new Wembley Stadium eventually opened in 2007, everybody was keen to play there – from the world's most successful international team – Brazil – to one of the world's most famous musical icons – George Michael.

The place was brand spanking new and the talk of the town, and either as a performer, sporting or otherwise, or as a spectator, a date with the new Wembley was seriously a box that needed ticking. And, in my capacity as the FA CEO and board member of Wembley National Stadium Ltd, I took real pleasure in seeing the venue come alive with an excited public who wanted to share a whole new experience.

Of course, there were issues to be dealt with – one important early one being that the pitch itself took some time to settle and involved a range of solutions before it got to be in a good place. I particularly thought it was imperative to get it right. After all, the Wembley pitch had been one of the defining factors of the original stadium.

As well as the annual set of major games to be held under the Arch, Wembley would also play host to matches to be played in the football competition of the London 2012 Olympic Games, having, of course, played a central part in the first post-war Olympics in 1948. On a personal level, firstly, as the FA boss, and subsequently when I left the organisation at the end of 2008, I was particularly keen to see 'my own team', Liverpool, play at the new Wembley.

It got frustrating – especially as all sorts of teams in all types of sports were making the new Wembley bow ahead of us, from the biggest names to some of the smallest. The list carried a remarkable cast list: England, Brazil (in their famous yellow shirts), Tottenham Hotspur, Aston Villa, Manchester United, Chelsea, Everton, Manchester City, Arsenal, Portsmouth, Stoke City, Birmingham City and Cardiff City … Ebbsfleet, Stevenage Borough, Dagenham and Redbridge, Barrow, Whitley Bay, Glossop North End, Coalville Town …

And St Helens, Wigan Warriors, Leeds Rhinos and Warrington Wolves from rugby league. The Miami Dolphins hosted the New York Giants at Wembley Stadium in NFL, and F1 world champion Lewis Hamilton drove his title-winning McLaren Mercedes around a figure-of-eight track set up in the stadium.

Even Muse, George Michael, Metallica and Take That beat world-famous Liverpool Football Club to playing at the new Wembley. As did the famous line-up that appeared at 'The Concert for Diana' held on 1 July 2007, which would have been her 46th birthday. It included members of the English National Ballet performing a scene from *Swan Lake*.

It was time for the Reds to regain their Anfield South squatting rights. And what is it that people say? 'I waited ages for a bus to come … and then three came all at once!' Liverpool fans experienced the football equivalent of that in the second half of the 2011/12 season – finally making their debut at the new Wembley over four and a half years after it had opened – and ended up playing there three times in almost 70 days. And it got the Reds back on the trophy-winning trail. Ironically, Liverpool's first opponents at the new Wembley Stadium were from South Wales – Cardiff City.

Part Two: Back to the Future

When Liverpool walked out of the tunnel alongside Cardiff City in February 2012 for the Carling Cup Final, it was worth reflecting that the Anfield club had experienced a fascinating blend of success and failure since last playing at the national stadium.

The Reds had still not won the league title since 1990 – almost unbelievable given their previous record, a wait of 21 years to that point, with many more years to come. They had won both domestic cup competitions in the Millennium Stadium, and produced one of the most historic comebacks in top-flight football when they turned around a 3-0 half-time deficit early in the second half of their UEFA Champions League Final with AC Milan. Famously, the Reds went on to win the match on penalties – a stunning win, and one that will be remembered fondly by Liverpool fans for decades to come, and the memories will be enshrined in one word: Istanbul. The two teams met again two years later in the Champions League Final, this time in Athens, this time the Italian greats coming out on top. But make no mistake, at this time the Reds were sitting at the top table in European football circles.

Off the field things weren't quite as simple, or successful, as a miscalculated selling of the club to two American businessmen, with ownership links into their own nation's major sports, caused havoc. In 2007, Tom Hicks and George Gillett, not business partners but old-time friends, combined resources to buy Liverpool FC, the club, at one stage, having seemed destined to be bought by suitors from the Middle East.

It was a change in plan that proved a big mistake, as it soon became apparent that Hicks and Gillett couldn't bring that Stateside sporting and commercial expertise over to the UK, and to own, understand and run one of world football's most prestigious sporting organisations – Liverpool Football Club. It was an uneasy and at times unmanageable situation: changes at board level, a lack of understanding of how football 'worked' and, critically, an unhealthy hostile relationship with the Reds' fans. The American duo made it seem very likely that the project would all end in tears – and an acrimonious conclusion to their tenure was duly signed off in the High Court in London on 13 October 2010, a story that was the lead on the BBC TV's ten o'clock news bulletin that auspicious day.

The club took up an offer to sell to another American company, New England Sports Ventures, whose principal, John W. Henry, expressed his pride on being confirmed as the new owners: 'We are committed first and foremost to winning. We have a history of winning and today we want LFC supporters to know that this approach is what we intend to bring to the club.' Working through their Fenway Sports Group, this set of Americans have delivered on that promise time and again, with only a rare wrong turn in the road.

Managerially, since 1996, there had been a reshuffling in the top job – very un-Liverpool like: Roy Evans; Roy Evans/Gérard Houllier; Gérard Houllier; Rafa Benítez; Roy Hodgson; and Kenny Dalglish, first as interim manager and latterly appointed as the full-time manager in 2011. The Liverpool managerial roundabout would kick in again in the summer of 2012.

On the field during this period the Reds bought Fernando Torres from Atlético Madrid, and he set Anfield alight by being a brilliant striker who could score every type of goal – often fed by Liverpool captain, and a Reds all-time great, Steven Gerrard. Torres and Gerrard were both heroic figures at Anfield, as was the likes of Jamie Carragher, who epitomised everything that was special about a player who gave his all to the Liverpool cause every time he pulled on the shirt.

On the final day of the 2011 winter transfer deadline, unexpected things happened quickly – the Reds' sharpshooter Fernando Torres made a shock move to Chelsea in a £50m deal. It is understood that he had been keen to make the transfer happen for some time. It stunned the Anfield faithful.

But Liverpool top brass didn't allow the enormous cheque to burn in their pockets. On the same evening, the club signed Uruguayan striker Luis Suárez from Ajax for £22.8m and then surprised everybody by splashing out £35m on Newcastle United's promising forward Andy Carroll. The Reds had effectively bought two players for the price of one.

It was a manoeuvre they played to great effect later in the decade when Brazilian star Philippe Coutinho left Anfield for Barcelona, and the money received from his transfer was converted into the stunning dual purchases of world-class Brazilian goalkeeper Alisson Becker and classy Dutch defender Virgil van Dijk. Back in 2011, the swift acquisitions of Suárez and Carroll delivered to Anfield one player who would become a legendary, if controversial, figure, the other a seemingly overpriced and injury-prone one.

Liverpool were now under the reins, on a temporary basis, of their iconic former player and manager Kenny Dalglish, who had been in and around the club as one of LFC's ambassadors and at the academy. And always a hero to the Kop, he heard his name chanted as the fans saw their team stutter.

Roy Hodgson's miserable short time in charge came to a close in the first week in January 2010 just six months into his tenure. After a poor start and a decisive defeat at Everton, eight games into the new league season the Reds were lying second from bottom in the Premier League, and Hodgson now owned the worst record of any Liverpool manager since George Patterson. It didn't improve that much and the likeable Hodgson, who never clicked with the Anfield crowd, moved on to pastures new. Liverpool FC executives made an urgent call to a cruise ship in the Middle East to invite club legend Dalglish, no doubt enjoying life on the ocean waves, to help them out of a deep hole and take on the manager's role, on a temporary basis, until the end of the season. He readily agreed. And later in the season he was confirmed as the full-time manager.

Sunday, 26 February 2012 – the Carling Cup Final

The wait was over. Some 5,738 days since Liverpool, with their players famously decked out in those controversial white suits, lost to Manchester United in the 1996 FA Cup Final, the club from Liverpool 4 were back at Wembley Stadium in a big domestic cup final.

Sure, they had enjoyed a profitable time at the Millennium Stadium in Cardiff and in Europe during that period, but it had been a frustrating wait for Liverpool fans to see their team play in the 'new' Wembley Stadium. And not just play there – but win there.

Looking ahead to the match, one famous former Liverpool player admitted he had his feet in both camps. John Toshack started his prestigious football career, which took him all over the world, playing for his hometown team, Cardiff City, back in the 1960s. Indeed, he made his debut for the Bluebirds at the age of just 16 years and 236 days – and went on to make 162 appearances, scoring 74 goals.

In November 1970, Liverpool came in for the tall Welsh striker, paying £110,000 for his services. Toshack became a fan favourite at Anfield and would go on to score 96 times in

247 appearances for the Reds – and play his part in league, FA Cup and European successes. 'When I was signing for Liverpool, Bill Shankly picked me up from Lime Street Station and growled, "You've come out of Sunday School now, son. It's the cathedral for you!"'

Toshack said about the Carling Cup Final:

> I would love to see Cardiff do well in the final. I was going to say it's a fantastic achievement for the team to get to Wembley but after the 2008 FA Cup semi-final and final, and the 2010 play-off final, the Cardiff players and their fans know their way around the stadium, whilst Liverpool will be making their first appearance at the 'new' Wembley.
>
> It is weird that Cardiff have more experience of the new Wembley and Liverpool have been to the Millennium Stadium more times than Cardiff! Liverpool must be desperate for a trophy, and I have to go for Liverpool. They've got all the big guns.

One of those 'big guns' was Luis Suárez. In many ways a flawed genius, brilliant on the ball, a scorer of stunning goals and a great team-mate – but with a streak of madness. In a home match with Manchester United in 2011, he was embroiled in a conflict with Patrice Evra. The United full-back accused the Liverpool player of using an unacceptable term. Suárez denied it, saying the term used meant something different in Spanish than it did in English – and the club defended him. Perhaps too fiercely for some.

The upshot was a 115-page report and an eight-match ban – and when the two teams met again at Old Trafford, Suárez didn't offer his hand to Evra as per the pre-match protocols. Again, the Uruguayan was criticised, and he and his supportive manager duly apologised for their part in the unsavoury episode.

Suárez looked to make his mark in a more positive way at the Carling Cup Final. 'As it is for all players, it is a dream to play at Wembley. It is going to be a special occasion for both teams. People in Uruguay know all about Wembley with it being the national stadium in England. It is famous worldwide.'

Kenny Dalglish's team selection for Liverpool's overdue return to Wembley Stadium was as follows: Pepe Reina; Glen Johnson, Martin Škrtel, Daniel Agger, Jose Enrique; Stewart Downing, Steven Gerrard, Charlie Adam, Jordan Henderson; Luis Suárez, Andy Carroll. Welshman Craig Bellamy, Jamie Carragher and Dutchman Dirk Kuyt would come on as substitutes during the match.

This match had a 'Liverpool win' stamped all over it, but the Welsh side, going along nicely in the Championship, were seriously up for the fight. And it was Cardiff City who scored first, Joe Mason notching for the Bluebirds in the 19th minute. It was just on the hour that Martin Škrtel finally pulled the Reds level from close range – no more goals were added in normal time. Extra time.

Liverpool finally got their noses in front in the 108th minute when substitute Dirk Kuyt, on for Andy Carroll, collected a rebound of his own shot at goal and drove it back into the Cardiff net. The Welsh side had played a full part in proceedings, and at times stretched Liverpool, for whom Stewart Downing was putting in a man-of-the match performance.

Just when it looked like Liverpool were home and hosed, Cardiff scored a late equaliser from a scramble following a corner, with Ben Turner on hand to score just two minutes from time. Penalties! And, amazingly, Liverpool's first two penalty takers, experienced and reliable stars, captain Steven Gerrard and Charlie Adam both failed to score. Things were looking bleak for the Reds.

Thankfully, Kuyt, Downing and Johnson hit the target – and Liverpool won the shoot-out 3-2. And with real irony, it was Steven Gerrard's cousin, Anthony Gerrard, having come on as a substitute, who missed Cardiff's vital fifth penalty. A bitter-sweet day for the Gerrard family.

An eighth League Cup for Liverpool, a place in the following season's European competition secured and there were two more visits to Wembley still to come.

Saturday, 14 April 2012 – the FA Cup Semi-Final

It was a super-busy early morning at Lime Street Station on Saturday, 14 April 2012, with trains arriving and leaving by the minute. Thousands of punters rolled into town from all over the country, past the statues of Merseyside favourite folk Ken Dodd and Bessie Braddock, before taking the local train, bus or taxi up to Aintree.

It was the 165th running of the Grand National – a national institution. A rejuvenated occasion with a packed crowd saw the 40 runners contest a course with less-severe fences, some of the jumps having been 'sanitised', post-race washdown and cooling areas for the horses created and there was just an all-round greater level of concern for the welfare of jockey and horse.

But it was still the Grand National – the greatest steeplechase on Earth – and suitably it was a horse named after another planet who took the honours in the closest finish in the history of the race. Neptune Collonges, a 33/1 French long shot edged out Sunnyhillboy, an Irish runner, with a remarkable burst to the line. The winning horse became only the third grey to claim victory in the race, the first since 1961 – and the winning margin must have been the width of a betting slip!

As folk piled into Liverpool early doors for a big day of racing, tens of thousands were heading out of the city to another English sporting landmark – an FA Cup semi-final. This one was between the two Merseyside giants, Liverpool and Everton. Both semi-finals were now being held at the new Wembley Stadium, largely because it made financial common sense to the governing body to claw back some of the money that had been spent building the stunning new arena – while recognising that some fans queried the decision as they thought it took away some of the 'magic' of reaching Wembley for the FA Cup Final itself.

Two points I would make are that, firstly, the in-stadium staging of the FA Cup Final and its status is significantly different to that of the two semi-finals – no marching bands, no formal pre-match protocols, no royal guests and no trophy lift at the end of the match, and, secondly, it almost guaranteed that everybody who wished to see their semi was able to gain access to the stadium. And another point, it is truly a neutral venue. So, to the match itself: 5/4/3/2/1 …

5 – To this point, Liverpool had five winning FA Cup finals at Wembley on their record – and hoped a semi-final victory over near-neighbours Everton would keep them on track to try to land a sixth.

4 – Liverpool and Everton had met four times in an FA Cup semi-final. In 1906, the Toffees came out on top, beating the Reds 2-0 at Villa Park. So, no double for LFC, having won the league that season. Meanwhile, Everton went on to win the FA Cup for the first time, beating much-fancied Newcastle United 1-0 – scorer, Alex Young. Next up was

March 1950, when goals from Bob Paisley and Billy Liddell clinched the Reds' victory over Everton at Maine Road. In 1971 the match was played at Old Trafford. Second-half goals from Alun Evans and Brian Hall were decisive for the Reds after an early goal from Alan Ball had given Everton a first-half lead. And in 1977 was the controversial semi-final played at Maine Road that went to a replay. Goals from Terry McDermott (BBC's goal of the season) and Jimmy Case put Liverpool in the driving seat before Everton levelled for 2-2, then saw Brian Hamilton's late 'winner' disallowed by referee Clive Thomas. The Reds won the Maine Road replay 3-0.

3 – The 2012 instalment of 'the Merseyside derby FA Cup semi-final' involved the strange story of *three* Liverpool goalkeepers. Liverpool's confirmed number one goalkeeper was Spanish star Pepe Reina, who Reds' manager Rafa Benítez had signed from Villarreal in 2005. Reina had been in goal when Liverpool beat West Ham United in the 2006 FA Cup Final in Cardiff. He had also been part of the Spain squads that won the 2008 European Championship and the 2010 World Cup. On 1 April 1 2012, Reina was sent off at St James' Park as the Reds fell to a 2-0 defeat. The keeper reacted angrily to being tripped up in his penalty box and thrust his head into the face of Newcastle defender James Perch. Contact was minimal but referee Martin Atkinson showed Reina a red card (his fellow countryman, full-back Jose Enrique, went between the posts for the last seven minutes of the match).

Up stepped Donieber Alexander Marangon, a Brazilian goalkeeper who played for both Corinthians and Santos in his home country, and Juventude and Roma in Italy. He signed for Liverpool as a deputy to Reina from Roma in July 2011. He made his debut for Liverpool against Aston Villa on 7 April, deputising for the suspended Reina – and, in his next match, then got a red card himself when conceding a penalty in the 25th minute against Blackburn Rovers. Two goalkeepers down, one to go … and just an FA Cup semi-final against Everton in front of a capacity crowd at Wembley to face!

Australian Brad Jones had signed for the Reds from Middlesbrough in 2010, then he went out on loan to Derby County before making his Premier League debut in that game against Blackburn Rovers, replacing the dismissed Doni. He saved the resulting penalty and was confirmed as the Liverpool goalkeeper for the big Wembley face-off with Everton. Jones had actually made his Liverpool debut in the Football League Cup against Northampton Town in September 2010, then followed up with a Europa League game against Utrecht in December of that year. In playing for Liverpool in the FA Cup semi-final, he would become the first Reds player to make his first four appearances for the club in four different competitions. He would later move to Bradford City.

2 – Despite Liverpool having played at Wembley just once since its 2007 opening, they faced opponents in Everton who had already played there in an FA Cup semi-final and final in 2009. The Blues had an FA Cup semi-final record of having played 24 matches, winning 13 of them. The Reds had been in 22 FA Cup semi-finals, also winning 13 times. Before the match, a minute's silence was held in memory of those who lost their lives at Hillsborough – and the annual Hillsborough Memorial Service was fittingly held the following afternoon at Anfield.

The referee for the game was Howard Webb, who had been chosen as the man in the middle for the 2010 World Cup Final between the Netherlands and Spain. It turned into a tough assignment, so perfect experience for a match between two neighbouring rivals!

1 – Everton's sole goal in the game came in the first half from Nikica Jelavić – and it is generally felt by loyal Evertonians that David Moyes's men had Liverpool on the ropes and should have gone for 'the kill'. They didn't – and missed a big opportunity, punished in due course by second-half goals from Suárez, who put the Reds level, and then Carroll scoring an 'inevitable' winner.

And Liverpool's number one, Brad Jones, turned in a very solid performance in such a huge contest and played 27 times for the Reds across a range of competitions before being released by the Anfield club in June 2015. Doni was also released by the club and went back to Brazil, where he retired from football following cardiac issues.

Saturday, 5 May 2012 – the FA Cup Final

It was yet another meeting between those two footballing giants, Liverpool and Chelsea – this time in the 131st playing of the world-famous FA Cup Final. These big-time fixtures between the two clubs were still coming fast and thick – with many more to follow.

Liverpool had won the Carling Cup, but Kenny Dalglish's men endured a miserable league season, eventually finishing eighth, while Chelsea had also finished outside the top four in the Premier League, but the Londoners had made it to the UEFA Champions League Final to play Bayern Munich in Munich.

It was also Chelsea's fourth FA Cup Final in five years, after beating Manchester United in 2007, Everton in 2009 and Portsmouth in 2010. Their previous victories in the competition were in 1970 with their replay win over Leeds United at Old Trafford 2-1, following a 2-2 draw at Wembley. They also won the last FA Cup Final played at the old Wembley Stadium, beating Aston Villa 1-0 – the goalscorer that day, Roberto Di Matteo, now the team's coach for the 2012 FA Cup Final.

Once again, my previous working relationship with the FA kindly gave me an invitation to the pre-match luncheon in the stadium's Wembley Suite and a seat in the Royal Box for the 2012 FA Cup Final, all of which I deeply appreciated and never took for granted. My earliest memories of visiting Wembley Stadium were standing on the terraces behind the goal at the Tunnel End, having hidden my precious ticket down the front of my trousers until I got to the turnstile but now I was properly suited and booted and sitting in the posh seats.

And, for me personally, this particular final was also an occasion that offered a clear window into the future. Three reasons – firstly, the FA Cup Final was moved from its traditional three o'clock kick-off time – in part to facilitate a set of Premier League fixtures earlier in the afternoon, and to give the final its 'own slot' on the day rather than, as in previous years, being the climax to the domestic football season and it having the whole final weekend to itself.

The move to a later kick-off time was supported, no doubt, by the broadcasters, including ITV and ESPN, who would be guaranteed a bigger TV audience as the majority of the match moved into the early evening. This was a controversial move, not helped by the fact that Virgin Trains had cancelled all services from the north-west that Bank Holiday weekend to carry out essential rail work, giving Liverpool fans the big headache of how to get down to London – and, just as importantly, how to get back home late on a Saturday evening.

The kick-off time being moved and the FA Cup Final not being protected as the big finale of the season was a sign of things to come – and a clear indication of where priorities now lay. And, sadly, part of a gradual chipping away at one of this country's great sporting institutions.

Next up, our old friend, the ubiquitous mobile phone, and its intrusion on the enjoyment of watching a live football match. Now I accept I may be something of a Luddite when it comes to modern modes of communication, but the chap I sat next to on the afternoon of the 2012 FA Cup Final spent the whole time on his phone – first telling all his friends where he was and how he had got there and then throughout the 90 minutes ringing them to check that what they were watching on TV tallied with what he had just seen himself in the stadium. Tedious.

And finally, a key incident in the game underlined the growing need for goal-line technology when, late in the match after coming off the bench, Liverpool substitute Andy Carroll, after pulling one goal back with some nimble footwork, looked to have scored a second goal, this time with a powerful header that would have levelled the scores at 2-2, only for Chelsea goalkeeper, Petr Čech, to pull off a miraculous save.

But did the ball cross the line? Referee Phil Dowd obviously didn't think so, neither did his assistant referee, but every time I watch it back now I believe what I thought at the time with my naked eye – that was a goal.

And the guy on the end of his mobile phone was telling all his mates that's what he thought too!

Added Time:

- Liverpool would beat Chelsea 4-1 at Anfield in the Premier League three days after their Wembley clash, and Chelsea coach Roberto Di Matteo's men would end the season as European champions for the first time, beating hosts Bayern Munich after a penalty shoot-out.
- And on 16 May, Kenny Dalglish lost his job as Liverpool's manager. His legendary status was

already secure, and, indeed, the depth of that respect would most positively be illustrated in years to come, including his being awarded a knighthood and having one of Anfield's stands named in his honour.

* * *

Wembley Stadium has been chosen on eight occasions to host UEFA's blue-riband event, the European Cup/Champions League Final, to date. In 1963, there was a midweek afternoon kick-off and a half-full stadium for the final between AC Milan and Benfica – the Italians taking the spoils with a 2-1 win. Brazilian Jose Altafini scored both Milan goals.

In 1968, Sir Matt Busby's ambitions were finally realised on an emotional warm London evening when his Manchester United team, with legendary team-mates Bobby Charlton and George Best playing starring roles, beat a Eusébio-inspired Benfica 4-1 after extra time to be the first English club to lift the European Cup. The triumph fittingly came ten years on from the Munich disaster.

The big final was back at Wembley in 1971 when the Dutch masters, Ajax, felled Greek champions, Panathinaikos, coached by the great Ferenc Puskás, who had graced Wembley himself in Hungary's famous 6-3 win over England in 1953. His Athens-based side lost 2-0, having surprisingly knocked out English champions Everton at the quarter-final stage.

Next up was 1978, when we will all remember Liverpool retaining the European Cup with a win over Club Brugge in a stadium simply swamped with Liverpudlians spread right around the ground. To adapt a famous line of BBC TV Sport commentator Barry Davies, 'Where are the Belgians … and frankly, who cares!'

In 1992, Barcelona finally got their hands on the European Cup when a late stunning free kick from Dutch star Ronald Koeman clinched victory over the Italian champions Sampdoria. A 'different' Barcelona were back at a 'different' Wembley Stadium in 2011. By this time, Pep Guardiola was the club's outstanding coach and maestro and Lionel Messi was pulling all the strings on the field. I still believe their 3-1 win over Manchester United was one of the finest performances of football I've ever seen. 'Magnificent' doesn't do it justice.

The 2013 UEFA Champions League Final brought Germany's great 'Klassiker' between the two footballing giants Bayern Munich and Borussia Dortmund together at the new Wembley Stadium. This match would have a significant place in the memories of Liverpool fans, as many of us were first introduced to a man who would have a huge influence over the Anfield club's welfare in years to come.

Michel Platini, UEFA President, had brought European club football's biggest match back to Wembley just two years after it had been last staged there, in recognition of the 150th anniversary of the formation of the FA in 1863.

Dortmund had begun to be a thorn in the side of their more famous Munich rivals, with Bundesliga titles in 2011 and 2012, and as DFB Cup winners, also in 2012. At Dortmund's helm was a remarkably talented coach who saw his role thus: 'What we can do is give people a distraction, make people happy … I cannot do anything to improve the political circumstances. I can't change anything about the social reality – but we can give these people a moment of happiness.'

The words sound familiar? The quote has echoes of the great Liverpool manager Bill Shankly, and the wonderful ability he had to emotionally charge a willing and hungry public. In fact, they were the thoughts of Borussia Dortmund's charismatic coach … a certain gentleman called Jürgen Klopp.

On the touchline at Wembley Stadium on the warm May evening of the 2013 Champions League Final, 45-year-old bespectacled Jürgen Klopp looked slightly uncomfortable in his formal dark-blue suit, his tie loosened around his neck and the top button of his new white shirt left wide open. And it looked like he'd had a haircut. He looked rather professorial, younger than his years, and stayed relatively still throughout the game. But in his own way he cut an interesting and imposing figure – he was memorable, he was different. And I remember thinking that at the time. He had the noisy devoted Dortmund fans eating out of his hands. The respect was mutual: 'The first time you come to our stadium, and you see 80,000 fans there, you think "Wow!" And it never becomes routine. You get the same rush every time you come here. It sends a shiver down the spine every single time.'

He would echo those sentiments about his similarly special relationship with the Liverpool fans and his love affair with the Kop in later years. Jürgen Klopp was the perfect fit for both clubs. His Borussia Dortmund team lost the 2013 final 2-1 to their German rivals, but he would lead his Liverpool team to three more Champions League finals – and beat Tottenham Hotspur in Madrid to land the much-sought-after trophy. The sixth time for the Anfield men – and what a reception he and his team received when they returned to the city on their unforgettable lap of honour.

The eighth and final time – thus far – the Champions League Final was held at Wembley was in 2024, with Real Madrid winning 2-0 over Jürgen Klopp's old club Borussia Dortmund. It was the Spanish club's 15th title. They remain one of world sport's most outstanding institutions.

* * *

Liverpool's next big match at the national stadium following their 2012 FA Cup Final defeat at the hands of Chelsea was three years later, in the spring of 2015. Now under the management of Brendan Rodgers, the Reds had gone close to finally landing the 'Holy Grail', the Premier League title, in the 2013/14 season.

At one stage of that season, they played 16 matches, winning 14 of them and drawing the other two. And the football the team played during this period was among the best seen for years. Without dwelling on it, the famous 'slip' from the Reds' inspirational captain, Steven Gerrard, in a dramatic match at Anfield against Chelsea (and Mourinho) in the run-in for the title gave the Londoners an important goal from Demba Ba, a lead that they doubled late in the game. It didn't deliver the title to Chelsea but, in due course, let in Manchester City. Rodgers's men finished runners-up.

The following season, 2014/15, marked the final campaign of one of the club's all-time finest players in Steven Gerrard. It is fair to say that at times he was a 'one-man' team. Liverpool's league form wasn't up to scratch – they finished sixth in the Premier League, having won just 18 of the 38 games.

They also went out of the group stage of the Champions League and lasted only one round of the post-Christmas action in the Europa League. It was left to the two domestic cup competitions for Brendan Rodgers's team to make an impact.

In the League Cup, the Reds were involved in a remarkable third-round tie with Middlesbrough – 2-2 after extra time, the teams were only split after a penalty shoot-out that lasted 30 spot kicks! It ended 14-13 to Liverpool, including successful conversions from the likes of Mario Balotelli (twice), Lucas (twice), Lallana (twice) and Suso (twice). He had scored in extra time as well. Raheem Sterling missed for Liverpool. The Reds were eventually knocked out at the two-legged semi-final stage by Chelsea (who else!), 2-1 on aggregate.

In the FA Cup, the Reds also reached the semi-final stage and another day out at Wembley. Their opponents on this occasion were Aston Villa, who they had comprehensively beaten in an FA Cup semi-final in 1996.

Philippe Coutinho gave Liverpool the lead. The little Brazilian had become the club's most outstanding player, so clever on the ball and with a real eye for goal. He was a special talent, who eventually left Anfield and Liverpool for the Camp Nou and Barcelona in the January 2018 transfer window for a colossal fee of £140m.

In a tight semi-final, Aston Villa hit back with goals from Christian Benteke and Fabian Delph – and the Wembley FA Cup Final 'ticket' was the Midlanders'. I happened to be on holiday in Dubai that week, but I soon got the magnitude of Villa's win from my son, Joe. A fanatical Aston Villa fan, he was whooping and hollering down the phone on a long-distance call to me at full time at Wembley. One very happy chap, good for him. Mind you, he was a lot quieter after Arsenal thrashed his favourites 4-0 in the FA Cup Final itself!

Added Time:

- I attended the Liverpool Players' Awards evening at the end of the 2014/15 season – and the loudest cheers that night were reserved for two former players who were the very foundation of Bill Shankly's Red revolution. Fifty years on from winning the FA Cup for the very first time. Ron Yeats, the captain that famous afternoon, and Ian St John, scorer of the winning goal that day at Wembley Stadium back in 1965, were given a rousing standing ovation. And rightly so.

Sunday, 26 February 2016 – The Capital One Cup Final

A poor start to the new season cost Brendan Rodgers his job – the Reds were lying in tenth place after eight games. Four days after Rodgers's departure, Jürgen Klopp signed a three-year contract with Liverpool Football Club, and a new era was about to unfold. Although it started with a 0-0 draw at Tottenham Hotspur, two impressive away wins at Chelsea and Manchester City gave Liverpool fans a new sense of confidence in the new man at the top.

One of the things that really struck home about Jürgen Klopp was his massive enthusiasm for his players, the fans and the club. What was also evident was his intelligent sense of perspective. Winning football matches was important, but other things mattered more. Klopp's first part-season with the Reds ended with them finishing eighth in the Premier League and out of the European qualification places. Meanwhile, Leicester City had surprised the whole football world by winning the Premier League.

The Reds went out in the fourth round of the FA Cup, but the club fared better in the League Cup under the 'latest' title of the Capital One Cup. Mind you, they got off to a sticky start. A seemingly easy third-round tie at home to League Two's Carlisle United looked a potential breeze, but it turned into something else. Despite having 47 shots on goal, the Reds could only draw 1-1 with the Cumbrian side, and with no further goals scored in extra time the match went to penalties. The Reds were saved the embarrassment of losing to lowly Carlisle by winning the penalty shoot-out 3-2. Hero of the hour was Liverpool goalkeeper Ádám Bogdán, who saved three Carlisle spot kicks – this on his debut for the club. The Reds beat Bournemouth 1-0 in the next round, and then produced a stunning performance in the fifth round with a 6-1 win at Southampton, including a Divock Origi hat-trick.

The two-legged semi-final with Stoke City was a tight affair, the Reds winning 1-0 away from home but then losing 1-0 at Anfield. The tie went to penalties and this time the Liverpool hero was another of their goalkeepers, first-choice Simon Mignolet, who saved spot kicks from former Liverpool striker Peter Crouch, and Marc Muniesa. Joe Allen wrapped up things for Liverpool.

Four rounds, two going to penalty shoot-outs – what were the chances of another spot-kick climax in the final against Manchester City? Liverpool's superstar Philippe Coutinho, relished the thought of a Wembley cup final: 'I'm very anxious to get out there and play the final. It's a great opportunity for me as an individual to get my hands on a first trophy for Liverpool and also for the club – four years waiting is too long. Liverpool have won many trophies in the past, but now it's time to end that break and we can kick-start the route back to success right here and now. It's our time again.'

Coincidentally, having written the above, I settled down to watch a bit of telly and stumbled into a programme on LFCTV featuring Coutinho's goals for Liverpool. It was a remarkable set of strikes that proved to be a timely reminder of just how good he was, especially in his time at Liverpool. 'He is an excellent player and intelligent': quite an endorsement at the time from none other than the incomparable footballing judge Pelé.

Perhaps strangely, after Coutinho left Liverpool he continued to play for major clubs such as Barcelona, Bayern Munich and Steven Gerrard's Aston Villa but rarely repeated the stunning form he displayed in front of the Kop.

Klopp's line-up for the Capital One Final: Mignolet; Clyne, Sakho, Lucas, Moreno; Milner, Henderson (captain), Can; Coutinho, Firmino, Sturridge. Early in the match, Mamadou Sakho got injured and was replaced by Kolo Touré, whose brother, Yaya, was playing for that afternoon's opponents. Two brothers on opposite sides in a big Wembley final was a genuine rarity.

Manchester City dominated the match for long periods and eventually took the lead shortly after half-time, Fernandinho's shot going under Mignolet's sprawling body. City had chances to put the game out of sight, with former Red Raheem Sterling guilty of missing two sitters. And Mignolet made amends for his failure to save City's opener with a series of super stops.

Late in the game, Coutinho scored from inside the Manchester City penalty area to square the match. Penalties! And the man who had played every minute of Manchester City's League Cup run, Joe Hart's understudy goalkeeper, Argentine Willy Caballero, became their unlikely hero. He made three vital saves – from Lucas, Coutinho and Lallana – and Yaya Touré secured a 3-1 penalty shoot-out victory for Manuel Pellegrini's men.

Three days later Liverpool would beat Manchester City 3-0 in the Premier League – goalscorers Lallana, Milner and Firmino. And the Reds would go on to play in the Europa League Final against Sevilla in Basle, where Sturridge gave Klopp's side a first-half lead, but the Spaniards scored three times in the second half to continue their dominance in this particular competition.

Klopp had made a positive start to life at Anfield but still needed 'runs on the board' to fully cement his relationship with the club's fanatical supporters, who were steadily warming to their new man and his new ideas.

Saturday, 9 August 2016 – the International Champions Cup

In June 2016, there was the one of the most important and tightest finishes in a nationwide contest, which had taken on a life all of its own. By the slenderest of margins – 52 per cent: 48 per cent – the people of the UK had voted to leave the European Union. The Referendum confidently called by Prime Minister David Cameron had thrown up a result he didn't expect. He resigned immediately.

'Brexit' had become the new word on everybody's lips, but the closeness of the result told its own story – and it wouldn't be until 11pm on 31 January 2020 that, two prime ministers on from David Cameron, Boris Johnson pushed through the high-level bureaucracy to take us out of the European Union. For good or ill, it was a decision that simply split the nation.

In the relatively gentler waters of sport, against all the odds, in football, Leicester City(!) won the Premier League title; Andy Murray was the world number one male tennis player and became the first person to win BBC Sports Personality of the Year three times; Team GB won 27 gold medals at the Rio Olympics and Mo Farah became the latest track star to achieve the long-distance double (5,000/10,000 metres) at the Olympic Games, joining greats like Zatopek, Kuts and Viren; and the appropriately named horse, Rule the World, was a 33/1 shot that won by six lengths in the 2016 Grand National.

Game of Thrones was by far the most popular TV show around the world in 2016, *Captain America: Civil War* the biggest film, and Drake had the best-selling single in the UK in 2016 with 'One Dance', enjoying 15 weeks at number one and certified triple-platinum by the British Phonographic Industry.

Euro 2016 had been disastrous for England under Roy Hodgson. They were knocked out in the round of 16 by Iceland! The English team were viciously mocked by the press, who described it as a 'second exit from Europe'. Roy Hodgson announced his resignation following the match.

Beware of the 'Big Sell'; that is, when some product, concept or idea is dressed up with a grand title and sounds more important than it really is. Let me introduce you to the grandly named International Champions Cup (ICC) – a multinational football competition built around a series of friendly association tournaments. It was an ambitious idea that came out of the USA, spread its wings across the world, had significant global media interest and by 2016 was putting on sets of matches in three distinct locations.

Australia hosted matches between Melbourne Victory, Tottenham Hotspur, Juventus and Atlético Madrid. China hosted matches between Manchester United, Manchester City and Borussia Dortmund. And the United States and Europe section involved ten clubs: Chelsea, Leicester City, Liverpool, Paris Saint-Germain, Bayern Munich, Inter Milan, AC Milan, Celtic, Barcelona and Real Madrid.

Founded in 2013, the make-up of the competition was changed virtually every year. Most clubs used this late July/early August tournament as warm-up games – friendlies but with a competitive edge and playing against clubs in their own peer group. It had its moments; for example, in the 2014 tournament, which also included Liverpool, a match between Manchester United and Real Madrid at the Michigan Stadium in Ann Arbor, Michigan set the all-time record for at a soccer game in the United States with 109,318 spectators.

The 2016 tournament schedule had Liverpool chalked up to play Chelsea and AC Milan in the USA. And then a week later the Reds would round off their participation in the tournament with a match against Barcelona back in Blighty at Wembley Stadium.

Two good friends, lifelong Liverpool fans Andy Proudfoot (author of the respected 'Red Watch' column) and brother Ross, and their partners, used the American leg of the tournament to follow the Reds and enjoy a sightseeing trip at the same time. Andy said:

I'm not usually one for pre-season friendlies but the prospect of spending a week or so in California while watching the Reds proved a temptation too far. And so we found ourselves in the iconic Rose Bowl in Pasadena, just outside Los Angeles, for the opening match of the ICC against Chelsea.

Frankly, the condition of the stadium left much to be desired, and the car parking arrangements on the adjacent golf course, with little signage or landmarks, saw many fans wandering the fairways looking for their transport hours after the final whistle.

The game was the usual fare, a 1-0 defeat with the likes of Ojo, Randall and Brannagan making appearances at some stage.

At least we won the second game against AC Milan at the Levi's Stadium in Santa Clara, just south of San Francisco. The Reds picked a stronger starting XI against a clearly rusty Italian side. The stadium itself was a significant upgrade from the Rose Bowl, just two years old and impressive in its scale. Origi and Firmino scored the goals in a 2-0 win. The Reds then flew off to St Louis for a friendly against Roma, who included Alisson in goal and Salah up front! We headed off to explore Yosemite, Death Valley and Las Vegas – a dream trip!

On Saturday, 6 August, a remarkable crowd of 89,845 filled Wembley Stadium for the International Champions Cup match between Liverpool and Barcelona – the Reds' final game in the tournament. It was the second-biggest crowd since the stadium had reopened in 2007. This 'friendly' occasion actually topped the crowd's partisanship shown by Reds fans at the 1978 European Cup Final against Club Brugge.

I would really invite readers to go on to YouTube and listen to the crowd's rendition of 'You'll Never Walk Alone' that late afternoon in August 2016. I've heard the anthem sung in all four quarters of the world – and it never … ever … fails to move me. And always will.

I was at Wembley Stadium for this match against Barcelona – still got the ticket: Block 552 Row 12 Seat 364, but lost in the midst of time was my memory of the singing of 'You'll Never Walk Alone' ahead of the kick-off. It is spine-tingling to hear virtually every one of the near-90,000 singing in unison and with such emotion and enthusiasm. Check it out.

The Liverpool team that afternoon included two new names that were going to play a huge part in the Klopp 'revolution'. Gini Wijnaldum had been transferred from Newcastle United to Liverpool in the summer of 2016. He was an outstanding £23m purchase and most Liverpool fans got their first look at the Dutch star as a Reds midfield player that afternoon at Wembley. He would make a much more famous and dramatic appearance against Barcelona as a second-half substitute at Anfield in the iconic 4-0 win over the Spanish giants in their Champions League semi-final three years later. His two goals that evening steered the tie firmly in Liverpool's direction.

Also on show at Wembley on that afternoon in 2016 at Wembley was Sadio Mané, who had been signed that summer from Southampton for a £30m fee. He would prove to be a magnificent acquisition and his deadly linking-up with Mo Salah and Roberto Firmino in future seasons was the stuff of legends. On a hot sunny day at Wembley, it was Mané who got the ball rolling, scoring the opening goal in the 15th minute.

In the second half the Reds went goal-crazy – former Liverpool star Javier Mascherano unfortunately scored an own goal to give his former team-mates a 2-0 lead in the 47th minute, and Divock Origi scored a minute later to extend the lead. He, too, would play a famous part in the debunking of Barcelona on that special European night at Anfield. A fourth, injury-time goal from Serbian Marko Grujić completed a rout – the 4-0 scoreline suggested that the Catalan giants, including their superstar Lionel Messi and ex-Liverpool legend Luis Suárez, were still shaking off the slumbers from their summer break, although they had beaten Celtic and Leicester City in games played in Dublin and Stockholm respectively, en route to their Wembley match-up with Liverpool.

For what it is worth, Liverpool were placed runners-up behind Paris Saint-Germain in the North America and Europe section of the competition. The concept ran until 2019, before the Covid pandemic kicked in and the men's version of the tournament never returned.

However, the growth of overseas friendlies, either tagged on to the end of a season or as a lucrative part of the build-up to a new season, is now just a firmly established part of the life of a major Premier League club – and certainly the visit of a major club like Liverpool to places like the United States, Australia and parts of Asia draws huge crowds, is commercially lucrative and underlines the growing reputation of the Premier League as the leading domestic competition in world football, and Liverpool's remarkable status in it.

Just switching sports briefly, I was also at Wembley on a night of unforgettable sporting action in April 2017, on a Saturday evening when Wembley Stadium looked an absolute picture as it staged the World Heavyweight Championship fight between Britain's Anthony Joshua and the former unified heavyweight champion, Ukrainian Wladimir

Klitschko. The ring walks were spectacular, bathed in laser lighting, the atmosphere with a post-war record crowd of 90,000 was electric, the broadcast being watched by an estimated 500 million people worldwide – and the bout itself, with Joshua's IBF world title and the vacant WBA (Super) and IBO titles also on the line, living up to its pre-match hype.

Both men were floored during the fight, but Joshua nailed his opponent twice in the 11th round and followed it up with a barrage of punches. With Klitschko trapped on the ropes, the fight was stopped, and Joshua declared the winner on a TKO (technical knockout). Later named by the respected *Ring* magazine as the 'Fight of the Year', it was a night when the new Wembley Stadium looked a million dollars, and the two brave fighters had truly earned their share of tens of millions of dollars.

October 2017/September 2018 – Spurs at Wembley

Wembley Stadium became the temporary home for Tottenham Hotspur while they built their new magnificent stadium – now the biggest club stadium in London – just a few yards from their famous old stadium, White Hart Lane. Tottenham's tenancy was only expected to last one season, but it went deeply into a second season. Wembley executives knew all about building delays and were happy to take the extended rent paid by the North London club.

In all, Spurs played nearly 60 'home' games across a range of competitions in the two seasons they 'lodged' at Wembley. Before the old Wembley was demolished, Arsenal had also used the stadium for two campaigns in the Champions League because of commercial restrictions at Highbury.

Liverpool visited Spurs at Wembley on 22 October 2017. I have the match programme for that Premier League game in front of me and, outside of a 'Spurs at Wembley' advert selling tickets for future matches, it paid very little reference to the fact that the game was being played in the national stadium other than the page with pen pictures of the Liverpool players being headed by the title 'Arch Rivals'. Neat.

A crowd of 80,827 watched Tottenham Hotspur put a defensively inept Reds to the sword. It was a comprehensive 4-1 win, two goals from Harry Kane and one apiece for Heung-Min Son and Dele Alli. Mo Salah was on target for the Reds.

The following season the Reds prevailed 2-1 in both the season's Premier League encounters. The first was at Wembley in front of a crowd of 80,188 in September 2018, with Wijnaldum putting Liverpool ahead in the first half and Firmino adding another in the second half. Of course, that wasn't 'business done' between Liverpool and Spurs that season. After legendary second-leg performances and results in their respective semi-finals, the Reds against Barcelona at Anfield and Spurs against Ajax in Amsterdam, the two English clubs locked horns in the biggest club game in world football – the UEFA Champions League Final.

The final was staged at the Estadio Metropolitano in Madrid on Saturday, 1 June 2019. The kick-off was 9pm local time, and Liverpool were ahead within two minutes of the start of the match, Mo Salah scoring from the penalty spot. The clinching goal came late in the second half from that scorer of 'important' goals, Divock Origi. It was the sixth time Liverpool had lifted that very special trophy and their return to a delighted Merseyside the following afternoon was truly memorable – with triumphant and celebratory scenes that will live long in the memory.

Two months later at Wembley, Liverpool would lose to Manchester City after a close tussle in the 2019 FA Community Shield, on penalties 5-4, after Jöel Matip's

77th-minute goal had squared the match following Raheem Sterling's 12th-minute opener for Manchester City.

Overall, it had been a memorable decade in which Liverpool had put themselves firmly back in the frame as European and domestic football 'royalty'. They added the UEFA Super Cup and the FIFA World Club Championship to their winning roster before the end of the year.

And Liverpool Football Club proudly ended the decade as European and world champions! As well as that special achievement, it was the decade that the Reds had reintroduced themselves to Wembley Stadium. Finally!

'Anfield South' was truly back in business.

Chapter 8

The 2020s … Will Play Chelsea!

Part One: An Old North vs South Rivalry!

On 7 September 1946, two Liverpool legends made their official Football League debuts for the Reds. Billy Liddell and Bob Paisley had signed for the Anfield club in 1939, and while they had played in wartime football, Liverpool's league match against Chelsea marked the real start of their illustrious one-club careers.

Gates were booming at football grounds all around the country – men back from fighting a war wanted to settle back into a more normal way of life. Watching their favourite football team play on a Saturday afternoon and being at Anfield cheering on their sporting heroes was all part of a Merseyside repatriation. The launching pad of both Liddell and Paisley's stellar careers was watched by a crowd of nearly 50,000 fans – and they witnessed Billy Liddell open his scoring account within two minutes of the start of the game.

At one point in proceedings, Liverpool, leading the London team 6-0, were seemingly strolling to a huge victory. Then in a brilliant second-half burst of four goals inside 17 minutes, Chelsea were seriously back in business. The Reds eventually ran out 7-4 winners in a fantastic 11-goal thriller – and George Kay's men went on to win the first post-war league championship.

A decade later, in 1958, BBC Television launched a Saturday afternoon sports programme that was to become as famous as the major events that were regularly featured within it. *Grandstand* became part of the social culture of the country, and every big sporting occasion and big sporting star featured in its celebrated lifespan of nearly 50 years.

One of its most fondly remembered sequences was the 'teleprinter' segment that filled the back end of the programme during the football season. As the afternoon's results chugged along a 'teleprinter screen' accompanied by the soundtrack of a PA news service printer, there was a real sense of drama. These were the days well before the instant recognition of a goal scored in any match, anywhere, any time, on multiple broadcast and social media platforms. Back then, the resolution of a match was often first seen as the result came into view on the famous BBC *Grandstand* teleprinter.

That iconic sports broadcaster David Coleman would fill in the gaps as the scores came up with details of the matches, league positions, etc. themselves. It was simple, engaging and brilliant television. It was eagerly watched by those people who wanted to know how their team had got on that afternoon – and by a huge number of more casual viewers who just wanted to know the results to check their pools coupons. And the device is still used in many different styles across many channels to this day.

One cold January afternoon in 1962, as a seven-year-old, I clearly remember watching *Grandstand* on our old black-and-white TV as the scores from that day's FA Cup third round popped up. I was waiting for one particular result on what was always considered a special day in English football's calendar.

'And here comes the FA Cup third-round result from Anfield,' said David Coleman with typical urgency. 'Second

Division leaders Liverpool … four … First Division strugglers Chelsea … three. And Liverpool were leading 4-1 in that game at one stage,' Coleman confirmed.

I remember it took an age to reveal Chelsea's score, but the Reds were through to the next round. The newspaper headlines told the story: 'Top Form Liverpool Just Good Enough – Chelsea cut back three goal lead.'

Two high-scoring matches, 16 years apart, between two of the great English football clubs from either end of the country – and a remarkable 18 goals shared by the teams in those 180 minutes.

Some 60-odd years later, Liverpool would meet Chelsea, now both English and European football heavy hitters, three times inside just three seasons in huge domestic finals at Wembley Stadium – twice in the League Cup Final, in 2021/22 and 2023/24, and the other occasion the FA Cup Final in 2021/22.

Three massive matches, with the whole world watching live TV coverage of the action from Wembley, and, remarkably, a total of 360 minutes of football played across the three finals – with just one goal scored, albeit a winning one for Liverpool. And a memorable pair of penalty shoot-outs. More of all of that in due course.

***

Returning nostalgically to the 1960s, I was reminded of how often Chelsea had figured in both Liverpool's rites of passage in that decade and beyond – and the personal adventures I had experienced with a fixture that always had a special ring of anticipation about it.

In 1965, of course, Liverpool had come off a 'toss of a coin' European Cup quarter-final win over German champions Cologne to beat Chelsea 2-0 in an FA Cup semi-final at Villa Park. Liverpool would go on to their famous first FA Cup Final victory against Leeds United at Wembley Stadium.

Then 1966 – two significant matches – Chelsea got revenge for the previous season's semi-final defeat with a 2-1 win in their FA Cup third-round tie with Liverpool at Anfield. 'The holders out!' barked David Coleman on *Grandstand*. On 30 April 1966, Tommy Docherty's 'Little Diamonds' clapped their Liverpool counterparts on to the pitch at Anfield on an afternoon the Reds clinched their second league title in three seasons. Chelsea boss Docherty had a huge respect for Liverpool manager Bill Shankly – both men having been Preston North End wing-halves during their distinguished playing careers.

A year later, September 1967, I had my first experience of being locked out of a big game, as my mum and I arrived at Anfield just as the paddock turnstiles were being shut ahead of that afternoon's early season clash between Liverpool and Chelsea. Although 53,839 fans made it into the ground that day, we didn't. I was 13 – and distraught.

The pre-match hype had all been built around new Liverpool signing Tony Hateley, playing against the club he had just left, Chelsea. He had played for them in the FA Cup Final at Wembley against Spurs earlier in the year. At a bouncing Anfield, a fired-up Tony Hateley put his former club to the sword, scoring two goals in two minutes early in the second half in a 3-1 win for the Reds. By this time, Mum and I were back home, rueing the fact we hadn't left earlier to get to the game, and, like a large chunk of the nation, we waited and watched the result pop up on *Grandstand*'s teleprinter. The consolation prize came that evening when, on a rare occasion, I was allowed to stay up late and watch Hateley's heroics on *Match of the Day*.

Another red-letter day between the two clubs came in January 1969, when Roger Hunt scored at Stamford Bridge to equal the Reds' old favourite Gordon Hodgson's league goalscoring total, with his 233rd strike of his career. Hunt would score a record-breaking 234th goal against Sheffield Wednesday a fortnight later.

Spin forward to 1986 and Liverpool beat Chelsea at Stamford Bridge on their way to that season's FA Cup Final – I was present at that game, and also there, of course, as Kenny Dalglish's men famously clinched the First Division title there in the same season, ahead of beating Everton in the FA Cup Final at Wembley the following week – the double secured.

And, in 2020, it was at Stamford Bridge again where Liverpool finally shook off their title-winning hoodoo that had seen them inexplicably not landing the big prize since 1990. This was the season that was 'put on ice' because of the Covid pandemic, which essentially stopped the world in its tracks and savagely hit communities through heartbreaking fatalities and serious illness. Football, like everything we all loved, was put on hold, as were many things in life, as overstretched hospitals up and down the country fought to save the lives of increasing numbers of people fighting the wilful effects of the pandemic. Lockdown hit all parts of society – and all sport was essentially closed down.

In 2019/20, Liverpool had been on a clear course to win their first league title since 1990 – and their first in the Premier League era – when the season was suspended in early March. It only resumed in June, with no spectators allowed in stadiums, and Liverpool buckled down and continued their pursuit of glory.

They got things underway again on my birthday(!) on 21 June, with a 0-0 draw against near-neighbours Everton behind closed doors at Goodison Park. This time, the elusive prize landed on an evening when the Reds weren't even playing! Instead, the squad and coaching team all gathered

Kenny Dalglish raises the European Cup at Wembley – his goal won the game for the Reds.

Liverpool's famous Scottish trio, Graeme Souness, Kenny Dalglish and Alan Hansen enjoy a private celebration after winning the 1983 Milk Cup Final.

Bob Paisley in his spiritual home – he was a multiple winner at Anfield South as well.

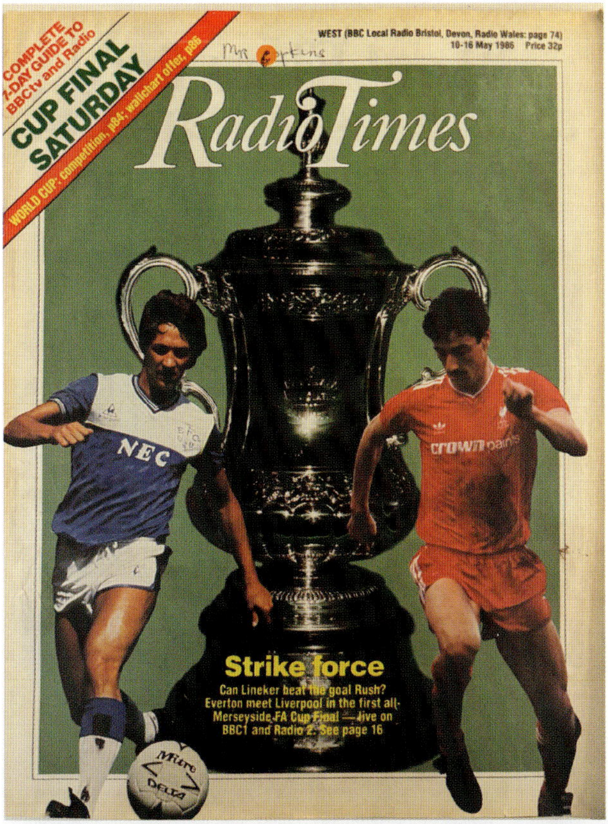

It's 1986, it's FA Cup Final Grandstand – and it's Everton v Liverpool

In a Rush – to share his big moment with the fans.

Three years on – and Ian Rush is still putting Everton to the sword.

'Macca' – a Wembley cracker – '92 and '95 – it's Steve McManaman

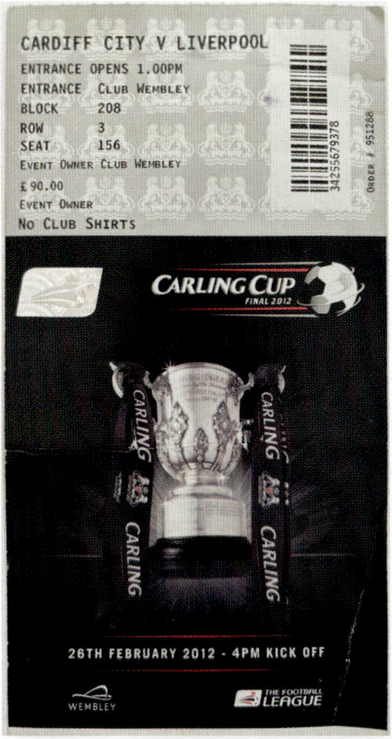

New Wembley – Old Routine, as Liverpool finally feature at the new 'Anfield South'! And the Reds take home the trophy after beating Cardiff City in a penalty shoot-out win.

2022 – Carabao Cup Final. Virgil van Dijk relaxes with the silverware.

'I feel great!' Jurgen Klopp gets that very special FA Cup Final-winning feeling!

'Let's hear it for the kids' – 2024 Carabao Cup success.

Arne Slot impressively took up the reins at Liverpool and despite losing his first tilt at a Wembley win, he is destined to have many special days there.

My spell at the FA included accompanying Prince William onto the pitch for his official opening of the 'new' Wembley Stadium in May 2007. A real privilege.

From standing on the stadium's terraces to sitting on the famous Wembley pitch itself (far right). Part of BBC TV's Grandstand team at the 1982 FA Cup Final. My job? To nab the winning captain before our broadcast rivals, do!

And the best bit – back at 'Anfield South' as a lifelong Liverpool fan with my eldest son, Jack. The Reds have just won the 2024 Carabao Cup. Thumbs up.

in a hotel back on Merseyside to watch as Chelsea beat Manchester City behind closed doors at Stamford Bridge on 25 June, and in so doing guaranteed the Premier League trophy was heading towards Anfield – at last.

On 22 July, Liverpool entertained Chelsea, behind closed doors, and the two teams entertained a big TV audience with a frantic end-of-season tussle with an old-fashioned high-scoring 5-3 win for the new Premier League champions – shades of 1946. Once the match was complete, the scene was reset inside an empty Anfield, and under the floodlights and spotlights, and after 1,156 games, club captain Jordan Henderson lifted the trophy – Liverpool were champions of England again!

***

The FA Community Shield in 2020 took place at Wembley Stadium on 29 August, just four weeks after Arsenal had beaten Chelsea in the delayed FA Cup Final. Man of the match in the final was Pierre-Emerick Aubameyang, who scored both goals in the Gunners' 2-1 win. This was the fourth time the teams had played each other in the FA Charity/Community Shield – Liverpool, winners with a famously impressive display in 1979, and again ten years later in 1989, while the Gunners took the honours in the domestic season's traditional curtain-raiser in 2002 and 2020.

But it had been an FA Cup Final and a Community Shield match with a real difference. They were both played in an empty stadium, due to Covid restrictions, and broadcast live on television with an artificial soundtrack of a noisy club-orientated committed Wembley crowd. These big matches, understandably played behind closed doors, underlined just how important fervently committed sets of supporters are, being essential in bringing a match to life and making it 'an event', especially one played in a stadium the size of Wembley.

In truth, I had little recollection of this particular match when writing this book. I don't even think an official programme was printed for it. But watching it back on YouTube, the match was 1-1 after 90 minutes, a brilliant goal by Aubameyang, levelled by Liverpool's Japanese striker, Takumi Minamino. The match went straight to penalties after 90 minutes, and Arsenal secured victory when Liverpool's young striker Rhian Brewster was the only player from either side to miss his spot kick in the scheduled five penalties apiece routine.

Added Time:

- Liverpool won the latest-ever league title – confirmed on 25 June.
- For the first time in their history, Liverpool beat every team in a top-flight season.
- The Reds set a new club record of 99 points in a season.

* * *

Liverpool's 2019 UEFA Champions League Final win over Tottenham Hotspur in Madrid had lined up a UEFA Super Cup match against Chelsea, who had beaten Arsenal in the Europa League Final. A bit of a 'curate's egg' of a competition, the Reds had previously won it three times, and their London rivals once.

The match, the first between two English clubs, was played in Istanbul at the home of Turkish club Beşiktaş, and it eventually spread over two days(!), with the match finally finishing at 12.43am on the second day.

The climax to a close-fought contest was a precursor to what would follow in the major matches between the two clubs at Wembley in the seasons that followed. Chelsea took the lead in the 36th minute, then Sadio Mané levelled for the Reds in the 48th minute. The match went into extra time, with Mané again on target in the 95th minute, but a converted penalty by Jorginho, given for a foul by Reds goalkeeper Adrián, making his full Liverpool debut, took the match into a penalty shoot-out.

Liverpool won the shoot-out 5-4, with the popular Spanish goalkeeper Adrián being the Reds' unlikely hero, saving Chelsea's fifth penalty from Tammy Abraham. Adrián had only been signed as a standby goalkeeper for Liverpool just days before the final. His name and picture weren't even in the match programme, but they led the back-page headlines in the English and Spanish papers the morning after the game.

'Awesome Adrian' ... 'Adrian-El Nuevo Hero!'

Added Time:

- Staged in the Khalifa Stadium in Doha, Qatar, in December, a goal from Roberto Firmino helped Liverpool beat Flamengo of Brazil to lift their third trophy in six months by winning FIFA's Club World Cup. Whatever the merits of the competition, it gave Liverpool the bragging rights to call themselves 'world champions'!

***

Part Two: Pandemic and Pandemonium

The pandemic had thrown many elements of everyday life out of kilter – and elite sport was no different. The 2020 Olympic Games in Tokyo were moved into 2021, and the UEFA's Women's Euros moved into 2022, while the Men's European Championships, Euro 2020, also moved on 12 months – and the original plan to play it over several different locations to celebrate the competition's 60th anniversary had to be adapted – as did the number of people who could attend the matches.

Both semi-finals and final of the competition were staged at Wembley Stadium, and the country was wildly excited about England's chances of winning their first major honour since 1966. Crowd sizes had been carefully controlled throughout the competition, with only 65,000 allowed for the England vs Denmark semi-final and just over 67,000 for the final itself.

Gareth Southgate's England had made it to the final and hopes were sky-high. Opponents Italy had Liverpool's 2024 recruit from Juventus, Federico Chiesa, in their ranks. Unfortunately, England were ultimately beaten in a penalty shoot-out, having taken the lead early in the first half, a lead that Southgate's team couldn't build a platform from. The game had ended 1-1 after extra time.

Unfortunately, too, the scenes before the match of ticketless fans trying to 'gatecrash' the occasion were simply a disgrace – and it was only good fortune that prevented this major incident from resulting in a more serious outcome with innocent people hurt or worse.

I went to the match with my two grown-up sons that day, and even though we got there some three hours before the kick-off, it was clear to me, with an experienced eye, that the build-up outside the stadium was menacing and largely made up of people who had been drinking heavily and for a long time, and who had ambitions to get into the stadium in any way they could. And hundreds did. Others just caused trouble.

It was a dark day for Wembley Stadium, and for the FA, and one that they were rightly heavily criticised for – as were the Metropolitan Police, for their perceived 'under-manning' of the event.

Little did we know that in the finale of the following season, thousands of Liverpool fans attending the UEFA Champions League Final against Real Madrid at the

Stade de France in Paris would be the innocent victims of a completely avoidable yet distinctly dangerous scene, as they legitimately tried to gain access to the stadium. All the problems were essentially caused by inadequate arrangements by UEFA and overbearing and aggressive policing by the French law authorities. Not a happy night. Both organisations tried to shift the blame elsewhere but were eventually brought to task.

Part Three: The Chelsea Trilogy

The late 2010s and the early 2020s will be remembered in football circles for the remarkable rivalry that pitched up between Liverpool and Manchester City. The Reds, under the leadership of Jürgen Klopp, pushed hard for the big prizes with their brand of exciting and 'hardcore' football, and City's brilliant, measured style under the genius of Pep Guardiola more than held its own.

It was a rivalry of the ages. Matches for the Reds against their M62 rivals, Manchester United, and their near-neighbours across Stanley Park still carried huge significance, but when it came to silverware, it was the matches at Anfield and the Etihad that tended to deliver the decisive moments.

But another elite match-up that had gone back many decades and spiced up the early part of the new millennium was the classic North vs South confrontation between Liverpool and Chelsea, who seemed destined to play each other at some stage of every competition they both entered. It was quite remarkable, and became a little bit inevitable, season in, season out. Boring perhaps.

Sunday, 27 February 2022 – The Carabao Cup Final: Chelsea vs Liverpool

And as we turned the corner into the second half of the 2021/22 season, Liverpool looked potentially on course for an unprecedented quadruple – the papers were full of it. Klopp's men were very well placed in the Premier League, although Manchester City still looked favourites, and the Reds were safely through to the knockout stages of the UEFA Champions League, had drawn Shrewsbury Town at home in the FA Cup third round, and had a two-legged semi-final with Arsenal ahead of them to secure a place in the Carabao Cup Final at Wembley. They were flying.

The Reds' route to the Carabao Cup semi-final had seen them need a late added-time equaliser from Japanese star Takumi Minamino to secure a 3-3 draw in their quarter-final clash with Leicester City, which took the game to penalties. Minamino actually missed his penalty in the shoot-out but goalkeeper Caoimhín Kelleher's two vital saves for the Reds did the trick in the spot-kick contest – and sent them into a two-legged semi-final against Arsenal.

Following a goalless draw at Anfield, Liverpool's 'Johnny on the Spot', Portugal's Diogo Jota, scored a brace, and the Reds were off to Wembley to play the reigning World Club and European champions, Chelsea. Both coaches were German, Jürgen Klopp and Thomas Tuchel, and the latter would be installed as England's new coach from January 2025. And both coaches relished the opportunity to meet in a big domestic final at Wembley.

Klopp: 'Cup finals are pressure games. But it is positive pressure. It is the pressure of opportunity. This sort of pressure is to be embraced. It is to be appreciated. There are 90 other clubs that would be desperate to swap places with us and Chelsea today. That's 90 sets of players and fans who would want to be where we are. How cool is that!'

Tuchel: 'A Wembley cup final is where every footballer playing in the UK wants to be, but I can assure you that even when I was young, growing up without the internet, and without the broadcast possibilities, to watch international games, being interested in football, you know what Wembley is.'

The scene was set for another intriguing clash between two sides who had shared those two draws in their Premier League clashes that season – 1-1 in August at Anfield and 2-2 at Stamford Bridge at the start of January. Third time up there had to be a winner!

But despite multiple efforts made by both teams, a combination of missed chances, near things, disallowed goals, wonderful goalkeeping by Chelsea's Edouard Mendy and Liverpool's Caoimhín Kelleher, plus a series of tight offside decisions, a brilliant, vibrant contest ended goalless after extra time. It was a great game. No goals, even after extra time, but a tremendous match.

Mendy, who put on a man of the match-type of performance, was controversially replaced by Tuchel in the dying embers of the game, for the Chelsea substitute goalkeeper, Kepa Arrizabalaga. Kepa had gained a reputation and had a positive record for saving penalties, triumphing in three of his four Carabao Cup shoot-outs – two of which had come in that season's competition, against Aston Villa and Southampton. A confident character, Kepa had made eight shoot-out saves in total in matches that had gone to that critical climax. Asked if he had managed to get some extra practice in ahead of the final, he said, 'I've practised more!'

Unfortunately for Kepa, it is unlikely he had practised *taking* a penalty …

The score in the penalty shoot-out was 10-10, no spot kick missed or saved, so it fell to the two goalkeepers to strike next. Mendy had looked crestfallen on the sidelines as the penalty shoot-out was taking place. Would Tuchel's decision to replace his first-choice keeper so late in proceedings be a match winner or a misjudgement?

Kelleher stepped up and calmly put his spot kick past his goalkeeping comrade Kepa. Cool as you like; 11-10. Then it was the turn of Chelsea's Spanish keeper, Kepa. He ran up and skied the ball about ten yards over the bar. More of a rugby conversion than a slotted penalty; 11-10. Game, set and match to the Reds.

The penalty kicks had been taken at the Liverpool end of the Wembley crowd. The fans there went absolutely mad as Kepa's kick disappeared into the North London night sky. Kelleher was mobbed by his Anfield team-mates – Klopp, delighted, praised the fans for their robust support.

Liverpool would leave the stadium with the Carabao Cup, a welcome guest on the team coach, and Jürgen Klopp's men were still on course for an unprecedented 'quadruple', with live chances of success in the Premier League, the FA Cup and the UEFA Champions League. One newspaper coined them 'the Quad Squad'.

Three days after the Carabao Cup Final, Chelsea owner Roman Abramovich put the glamorous West London club up for sale. Russia's invasion of Ukraine and potential sanctions on UK-based Russian oligarchs by the British Government made Abramovich's ownership of the club simply untenable. A club he had bought for £140 million from Ken Bates in 2003 was eventually sold to a consortium led by American billionaire Todd Boehly, for £4.25 billion. They were buying a club that had become serial winners – 19 major trophies landed during Abramovich's time at Stamford Bridge. It was made clear that a huge chunk of that money would be spent on relief work stemming from the Ukraine-Russia war.

I met Abramovich several times over the years, and he was always polite, but was a man of few words. Perhaps the most significant moment was when 'his Chelsea side' played Manchester United in the 2008 UEFA Champions

League Final held in his native Moscow. The Blues lost 6-5 on penalties, and I bumped into a very crestfallen Chelsea owner, literally seconds after the last penalty had been taken – my words of condolence were duly noted by him before he drifted away, a man very much with his own thoughts that evening.

Meanwhile, next up at Wembley Stadium for Liverpool was a 2021/22 FA Cup semi-final against Manchester City. It doesn't get any easier, does it. Liverpool and Manchester City were going at it again full pelt for Premier League supremacy. They were streets ahead of their top-flight rivals and were almost playing in a league of their own.

Chelsea had drawn the easier task in the FA Cup semi-finals, playing their London rivals Crystal Palace and winning comfortably 2-0, but all eyes were on the other tie: Guardiola vs Klopp; Manchester City vs Liverpool.

The Reds got off to a flyer in front of nearly 74,000, with a headed goal from Konaté, then Sadio Mané benefitting from a desperate mistake from City's stand-in goalkeeper, Zack Steffen, put Liverpool two up on 17 minutes before he added a third in first-half added time. Jack Grealish pulled one back two minutes into the second half, and Liverpool missed several opportunities to put the game to bed before Manchester City's Bernardo Silva added an added-time goal – too little, too late.

***

Just 76 days after playing Chelsea in the Carabao Cup Final, the two teams would meet up again – this time in the Emirates FA Cup Final – the occasion celebrating the 150th anniversary of the first FA Cup Final. A sporting contest with a marvellous history and heritage – and one that's loved the world over. The first final was a match was between Wanderers and Royal Engineers played at the Kennington

Oval in 1872, when 15 teams had entered the inaugural competition, although only 12 played in it.

Wanderers' berth in the final had been achieved with a bye – after Scottish opponents Queen's Park – exempted until the semi-finals – couldn't afford to stay in London for a semi-final replay.

Morton Peto Betts, a member of the FA Committee, wrote himself into football folklore by scoring the only goal of the final, played in front of a crowd of 2,000. Wanderers' captain, FA Committee member, Charles Alcock, the gentleman who actually came up with the original idea of a knockout competition, lifted the first FA Cup – a silver trophy purchased for £20 and nicknamed 'the little tin idol'.

* * *

If the FA was celebrating the 150th anniversary of the first FA Cup Final, it got me thinking ahead of the 2022 FA Cup Final between Liverpool and Chelsea just how indelibly linked I was to English football's 'blue-riband' event. And that it had been something of a 60-year love affair!

A month away from my eighth birthday, I watched my first FA Cup Final on the BBC on a black-and-white TV, all the way back in 1962 – Tottenham Hotspur, who had won the final in 1961, beat Burnley 3-1 a year later. I then 're-enacted' the final on our lounge carpet with an old set of Newfooty players, the precursor to the legendary Subbuteo, which had been given to my dad by a workmate. I worked out that since that afternoon, I've seen virtually every FA Cup Final – and across what must be a unique set of roles.

Young armchair TV viewer in the 1960s – in place from 11am in the morning; teenage 'debut' at Wembley for the '71 final; a Wembley spectator at four more finals in the 70s, two courtesy of old schoolmate Manchester United's

Steve Coppell; the 1980s and 1990s, every final in a variety of positions for BBC Sport, including that of being editor of *Match of the Day*, but by far the most fun of those various roles was for about five years being sat five yards from the goalposts at the Tunnel End for the duration of the matches; early 2000s attending as ITV's Controller of ITV Sport at matches chiefly played in Cardiff; 2005–08 as CEO of the FA, taking part in all the pre-match protocols, including 'meeting the teams' ahead of the 2006 final between Liverpool and West Ham United; then the much-heralded return to the new Wembley Stadium in 2007.

For the last 15 years or so, either as a guest of the FA or as part of the wider football 'family', and then from 2022 back in my rightful role as a genuine fan of the game, the FA Cup Final has been part of my personal and professional life. Over those years I reckon I've only missed two finals, either live in the ground or on TV – the 2014 match between Arsenal and Hull City, and the following year's final between Arsenal and Aston Villa. On both those occasions I was on duty elsewhere as Chair of the Rugby Football League.

Of the 15 FA Cup finals Liverpool have been involved in, I've seen 12 of them live. I wasn't around in 1914(!) or for the Reds' debut at Wembley in 1950, and I watched the team's great (greatest?) day in 1965 on TV. But since 1971 I've had the privilege, pleasure and occasional disappointment of watching my club competing in the FA Cup Final.

I continue to see the FA Cup Final as an essential part of English football's heritage. For sure, it has lost some of its unique appeal, with the growth of emphasis on the Champions League and the Premier League, but we have something that's the envy of the world, and something that has been copied in all parts of the globe. But our competition remains the original and, for me, the best.

Thank you, Mr Alcock. What a good idea you had!

* * *

Saturday, 14 May 2022 – the Emirates FA Cup Final: Chelsea vs Liverpool

Jürgen Klopp's impact on Liverpool Football Club's status and honours board can never be doubted. The brilliant German's tactical know-how, his inspirational nature and his connection with the Reds' fans was unrivalled – and he had already cemented his place in Anfield folklore.

However, his record in the FA Cup during his time at the club was, at best, ordinary. In the nine seasons he competed in the competition, the form that was clearly shown in their Champions League and Premier League exploits wasn't matched by his record in the English football's most admired cup competition … 2015/16 knocked out in the fourth round; 2016/17 fourth round; 2017/18 fourth round; 2018/19 third round; 2019/20 fifth round; 2020/21 fourth round; 2021/22 winners; 2022/23 fourth round; 2023/24 sixth round.

Klopp personally addressed the issue in the 2021/22 cup final matchday programme:

> To avoid any doubt, I absolutely love the competition. I recognise its importance in the club's history and how much it means to our supporters. And at the beginning of the season, I am desperate for us to give all we have to try and be in the final in May. With a chance of winning it.
>
> This season, we have achieved the first part of that aim. We are here today in the final! Really cool.
>
> For the thousands who have travelled at great expense to back our team today I can only say on behalf of the team how appreciative we are. We

> are always humbled by it. We never take it for granted. These are the days when we are allowed a bit of nostalgia. I am not an expert in these things, but I know people who are, and they tell me the 1965 FA Cup Final was one of the most important days in our club's history.

The team he picked for the occasion showed three changes from the one he had fielded against Chelsea in the Carabao Cup Final in February. Alisson was restored in goal, Konaté came into central defence, replacing Matip, and Thiago, who had missed out on a starting place in the Carabao Cup Final after sustaining an injury in the pre-match warm-up, was back in midfield, replacing Fabinho.

The Reds' route to the final had taken care of Shrewsbury Town, Cardiff City, Norwich City, Nottingham Forest and Manchester City ... and now familiar rivals Chelsea stood between them and their eighth success in the FA Cup. Astonishingly, like the match played in February between these two sides, the much-anticipated game ended goalless after extra time.

Once again, the match defied most people's usual critique of a 0-0 draw as being a disappointment. There was plenty of chances for both the Reds and the Blues, but none taken. The woodwork was also rattled, but on a hot sunny Wembley afternoon in mid-May it was time for a penalty shoot-out. Another penalty shoot-out!

Chelsea got it off to a positive start through the experienced Marcos Alonso, matched by Liverpool substitute James Milner; 1-1. The Chelsea club captain, Cesar Azpilicueta, then missed his penalty, and Thiago scored for the Reds; 2-1. Reece James levelled the score at 2-2, before another Reds substitute, Roberto Firmino, nudged Liverpool ahead 3-2. Former Everton star Ross Barkley then stepped up for the London side and made it 3-3. Trent Alexander-Arnold, 'the Scouser in our team', made it 4-3 to the Reds, only for Jorginho to make it 4-4.

Sadio Mané then had his penalty saved by Edouard Mendy, and Chelsea went ahead through Hakim Ziyech; 4-5. Diogo Jota, a first-half substitute for the injured Mo Salah, squared things at 5-5. Now to the sharp end of the contest, Mason Mount, 23, had his penalty brilliantly saved low to his left by the Brazilian super-keeper. Still 5-5.

And up stepped a very unlikely hero – Liverpool's Greek full-back, Kostas Tsimikas, the club's 'funny man', and often cover for Andy Robertson, as he had been on this day at Wembley. He walked up slowly to the penalty area, then put the ball into the back of the Chelsea net before running off in joyous celebration, chased by his victorious team-mates.

In all, four of Liverpool's penalties had been scored by Klopp's substitutes, Milner, Firmino, Jota and match-winner Tsimikas, who had only been on the field nine minutes of the 120 played. Liverpool's mass of fans, who had drawn criticism from some quarters for their widespread lack of observance of elements of the pre-match protocols, were ecstatic.

Goalkeeper Alisson: 'It was amazing ... such a great performance. We didn't score in normal time but it was a proper fight in extra time. The boys were unbelievable in scoring the goals. I just needed to save the last one.'

A second trophy in the bag, the unlikely quadruple still on. And by the time the season would end, Liverpool had played in every match possible across all competitions.

Added Time:

- Liverpool's quest for the quadruple went to the final day of the Premier League season. A point behind Manchester City, the Reds needed to beat Wolves at Anfield and hope Manchester City failed to beat Aston Villa at the Etihad. At one point Liverpool were drawing 1-1 with Wolves, who had taken an early lead, and City were trailing 2-0 to Villa – a situation that got the crowd very excited, if briefly, at Anfield. In due course, Manchester City got ahead of their Midlands opponents, scoring three goals in a six-minute burst, and they stayed ahead to the final whistle. Liverpool completed their league season with a 3-1 win over Wolves.

- Pep Guardiola's men had won another Premier League title and pipped Liverpool again by a single point: 93 to 92. And the Reds would go on to lose the UEFA Champions League Final, 1-0 against Real Madrid in Paris – an event completely marred by UEFA's ineffective planning and the French authorities' underwhelming and overbearing matchday management of the impeccably behaved Liverpool supporters.
- Liverpool and Manchester City would meet in the 2022 FA Community Shield, held at Leicester City's ground in late July, Wembley being used to host the UEFA Women's Euros 2022 Final. The Reds won the Community Shield match 3-1.

Sunday, 25 February 2024 – the Carabao Cup Final: Chelsea vs Liverpool

A late fitness test. All part and parcel of a footballer's life on the morning of a big game. Players determined to make it to the kick-off, the coaching and medical team assessing the risk – to the player, to the team and to the potential result.

I've witnessed plenty of these last-minute 'check-ups', quite often made on stretches of grass behind the overnight hotel – and have been amazed at how simplistic they can be or, conversely, how scientific they are. It is, however, a rare occurrence when a fan takes a late fitness test – not for hell nor high water will a dedicated supporter miss a game, and certainly not a big one. That was my dilemma hours before the 2024 Carabao Cup Final between Liverpool and Chelsea.

A dodgy late Friday night fish supper had resulted in me spending most of the following eight hours on or near the loo. I had food poisoning. I spent most of Saturday in bed with a high temperature, avidly reading all the newspaper previews of the Carabao Cup Final, while never being more than a few strides away from an increasingly desperate trip to the bathroom.

At risk, a trip to Wembley Stadium to see Liverpool's latest head-to-head with Chelsea, the club with an ever-revolving door welcoming their latest new manager through it, while hustling the previous one out of it. It was also potentially going to be Jürgen Klopp's final Liverpool match at Wembley. His decision to leave Anfield, after a stellar time putting Liverpool back where they belonged, was now public knowledge, and we all wanted to cheer him through his final few months. Food poisoning or not. I had bought two expensive tickets for the match, £150 a pop(!), and my son, Jack, and I had been looking forward to the game for several weeks.

Sunday morning, temperature down to normal, visits to the loo gradually reducing, things looked promising for us making the three o'clock kick-off. I still hadn't made up my mind. It is one thing for the national stadium to boast about having 2,618 toilets – but how close, and appropriate, would the one nearest our seats be? And what if the blasted fever came back midway through the first half? Man, or mouse?

I rang Jack and told him I had declared myself 'fully fit' for attending the match. My wife, Gerry, a long-suffering football agnostic, said, 'You're mad ... watch it on the box in our nice warm lounge.' My lad, Jack, said, 'Great, Dad, I knew you'd make it! But bring plenty of loo paper just in case.'

Decision made.

For the Reds' 'Mr Cool' defender, Virgil van Dijk, it was a special moment. As captain he was leading out his Liverpool team in a cup final at Wembley for the first time:

> It is always special to be back at Wembley and to play in a final, but, of course, I'm very excited to lead the boys out and that does mean something a little bit extra.
>
> As captain, you represent Liverpool. That's not just at the training ground or on the pitch during matchday, it's all over the world. I feel the responsibility – I embrace it and enjoy it. On the pitch, I'm very vocal. I'm always shouting and organising. Outside of the pitch, I just want to keep natural. If someone needs help or is going through a difficult moment, or needs a kick up the backside, then I will be there.

Liverpool's squad looked significantly different than in recent seasons – no Henderson, Firmino, Mané, Milner, Oxlade-Chamberlain and Keïta, and, during the latest campaign, lots of young players had been given an opportunity to shine.

In reaching the final of the Carabao Cup, Liverpool had actually fielded 24 players – with only goalkeeper Caoimhín Kelleher having played in every minute of their five Carabao Cup ties. Four teenagers had been given match-time in the Carabao Cup up to the final – Ben Doak, Bobby Clark, Luke Chambers and Stefan Bajcetic. Another two teenagers would be added to that list before the cup final itself was over – James McConnell and Jayden Danns. And 20-year-olds Conor Bradley and Harvey Elliott were also in the starting line-up.

In the programme for the Carabao Cup Final, Trent Alexander-Arnold had answered a standard A-Z questionnaire about his time at the club, his best mate there and other elements of his footballing life, etc. He would miss out in the game through injury, but on the question of 'Mystery – Tell us something we might not know about you …', his answer: 'I know how to solve a Rubik's Cube.'

The biggest puzzle the two sides meeting on that cold February afternoon had was how to score a goal against each other. In their two recent cup finals they had played 240 minutes of football, both full of near misses, without bagging a single net-buster. Both matches had gone to penalty shoot-outs. Astonishingly, it would be another 118 minutes before that 'curse' was finally put to bed in this final, with another penalty shoot-out looking inevitable.

Liverpool made seven changes from their starting line-up in the 2022 FA Cup Final for this match, some forced through injury. Chelsea, who had been on a much-criticised spending spree, under new ownership and new management, with Mauricio Pochettino now in charge, had a completely different starting XI than the one that had kicked off the FA Cup Final less than two years before.

Jürgen Klopp summed up his own emotions ahead of his latest big match at Wembley:

> The football moments speak for themselves, and we will hope for more of those today, but just as strong are my recollections of the crowd – the colour, the passion, the noise. That we could do it again is a privilege that I could never take for granted.

As the players emerged from the Wembley tunnel, Sky Sports football commentator Peter Drury set the scene perfectly with his usual verbal panache: 'Red and Blue, North and South, Albert Bridge and Albert Dock – so much separates them, and yet so frequently their modern histories collide.'

The match went end to end, Kelleher in typical fine form. On the hour, Virgil van Dijk seemed to have finally broken the seemingly interminable goalless deadlock with a fine headed goal. Only for VAR, after a lengthy period, to call referee Chris Kavanagh to the screen. An offside decision went against the Reds. Back to 0-0.

It was in extra time, in the 118th minute when Liverpool finally secured their tenth League Cup victory, with another towering headed goal from captain Virgil van Dijk. This time, from a Tsimikas corner, Van Dijk's brilliantly judged header soared past the Chelsea keeper, Petrović. Cue pandemonium in the stadium – at the Red end and on the team benches hosting the Liverpool contingent of players, coaches and staff.

The clock ran down. The final whistle was blown and, again, Drury found the words to sum it up perfectly: 'The ribbons are red! The Klopp kids, the Kop kids, have won the cup.'

The main man, Jürgen Klopp, celebrated joyously – and, especially, shone with pride at how the youngsters on the pitch had delivered for their club. And the Liverpool fans were in fine voice, ecstatic at the latest trophy in Klopp's remarkable triumphant spell at the club. 'The best of the lot' was his emotional take on proceedings.

And, as a Liverpool supporter, who first watched his favourite team back in 1961, I can tell you it was a personally emotional moment to see a team – my team – a mixture of thoroughbreds and young colts win at Wembley again. The Arch, brightly lit in red, letting the world know Liverpool were in the trophy-winning business.

And at Wembley. The national stadium. Anfield South. You never know when the next time will be.

Added Time:

- Dutchman Arne Slot took over the managerial hot seat from Jürgen Klopp at Anfield in the summer of 2024 – and the former boss at Feyenoord has made a terrific start to life at LFC.
- Slot's cool, calm demeanour, coupled with his shrewd assessment of the club's playing staff, admittedly a strong one left behind by his predecessor, led to a remarkable run of results in his first season in English football. His tactical awareness, team rotation and clever use of substitutes took the Reds well clear of the field on an exciting journey to land the club's 20th league title.

  On a beautiful late Spring afternoon, and in front of an expectant and wildly excited Anfield crowd, Slot's men trounced visitors, Tottenham Hotspur, 5-1 to clinch their landmark 20th title.

  The post-match celebrations were memorable, including a genuinely classy moment when Arne Slot returned the compliment of his predecessor by leading the Anfield faithful in a chorus of 'Jurgen Klopp, Jurgen Klopp…'

  It was a fantastic day and an outstanding achievement for everybody connected with Liverpool FC.
- In other competitions winning blitz of results in the newly shaped UEFA Champions League competition sent the Reds confidently into the post-Christmas last-16 knockout stage. A titanic two-legged battle with French champions, Paris Saint-Germain, ended with the Reds falling the wrong side of a second-leg penalty shoot-out at Anfield. It had been a breathtaking pair of matches – exhilarating and exhausting.

- In the FA Cup, Slot's decision to leave many of his front-line stars at home for their fourth-round tie at bottom of the Championship Plymouth Argyle left the boss more red-faced than enjoying another red-letter day, as the Anfield club fell victim to the game's oldest cup competition's ability to land giant-killing after giant-killing. Plymouth Argyle 1 Liverpool 0.
- Slot enjoyed greater success in the Carabao Cup, with his team steaming through four rounds on the road to Wembley, using 27 players en route. Round by round: Liverpool 5 West Ham United 1, Brighton 2 Liverpool 3, Southampton 1 Liverpool 2, before a two-legged 4-1 aggregate win in their semi-final against Tottenham Hotspur. They had nailed it. And so to Wembley Stadium on a cool late sunny March afternoon for Slot and his Liverpool team.
- Ten-time winners of the League Cup, Liverpool were warm favourites ahead of their opponents, Newcastle United – still in their search of a first domestic trophy since winning the FA Cup in 1955. It had been a long wait for silverware for the football-mad Geordies. Their last winning final captured on 'black-and-white' film for the Black and Whites.
- A little bit of personal stuff now. My son, Jack, married into a fanatical Newcastle United family – real lifelong supporters – so there was a lot of friendly family rivalry knocking around ahead of the big game. The Newcastle 'side' of the extended family 'hoped' rather than expected their team would win, while we, the Barwicks, quietly expected to triumph, but never overplayed our hand. We had been there before.
- On the big day, Liverpool made their 45th appearance at Wembley Stadium, 31 of them at the 'old' version of the national stadium, the rest under the iconic Arch.

The sights and sounds on that afternoon contrasted the colours of Liverpool's army of fans regaled in red and white, and the Newcastle end of the stadium sharply alive with strident black and white favours. Cutting to the chase, it proved to be a great day for the Geordies. Their long-awaited 70-year pursuit of domestic silverware was finally over.

- Their 2-1 win over Liverpool was well deserved, no arguments, and even a late goal by Federico Chiesa couldn't save a disappointing day for the Reds. And the remarkable scenes at the end of the game showed just how much it meant to the travelling fans from the North East.
- On this occasion, Liverpool and their huge following would have to lick their wounds. It wasn't their day. But, as this book has clearly illustrated, there have been plenty of 'Wembley Days' for Liverpool Football Club in the past, and for sure there will be plenty more to come in the years ahead.
- After all, Wembley Stadium isn't dubbed 'Anfield South' for nothing!

Chapter 9

Memories, Matches … and Magic!

I RECENTLY had the pleasure of sitting next to Sir Kenny Dalglish at a charity event we were both supporting. I've known the great man for many years and always enjoy his company. During the evening, I told him I was writing a book on Liverpool Football Club's many games played at Wembley Stadium – both the old stadium and the new one.

Sir Kenny had both played and managed many matches for the Reds there, including making his debut under the Twin Towers in the 1977 FA Charity Shield game against Manchester United. Over a glass or two of good red wine, we discussed many of those occasions and I asked him to pick out one that was the most memorable. I did tell him it couldn't be a Scotland match!!

He had a wide choice, of course, not least the match against Club Brugge in the 1978 European Cup Final, when he scored the brilliant winning goal via a pass from his great mate, Graeme Souness, securing the Reds' second triumph in world football's most famous club competition. Kenny eventually settled on the two Merseyside derbies in the FA Cup finals of 1986 and 1989 – the first, as player-manager, which clinched Liverpool's double, edging out their near-neighbours in a remarkable climax to the season.

He talked about the great evening he and his team-mates, friends and families had enjoyed after the match and their unforgettable return to Liverpool – and the reception that both teams got as they went around the city the following day.

The Liverpool legend, then as manager, ultimately chose the 1989 FA Cup Final against Everton three years later as the most significant match he was involved with for Liverpool at Wembley. 'It was one we *had* to win,' he said. He didn't need to explain why.

In the aftermath of the horrendous Hillsborough disaster, it was the clear that the players, management and club officials knew victory in that match would, in some way, honour the memory of those who had perished on that fateful day in South Yorkshire. And Sir Kenny and Lady Marina Dalglish have been an ever-present source of support and care for the families and friends of the deceased ever since. They are special people.

Many other people, from all walks of life, have told me their own memories of the special days they have spent watching the Reds play at Wembley Stadium. And why.

Here is a fascinating collection, written in their own words.

Ross Proudfoot – Lifelong Liverpool Fan: 1965

What a time it was to be a teenager in Liverpool in the 60s. Born a mile and a half from Anfield, I had been brought up watching Liverpool Schoolboys before performing the rites of passage: Boys Pen, Paddock, Annie Road End and Kop.

I'd seen Kevin Lewis score twice against Southampton to get us back into the First Division at long last but, as the FA Cup was the 'Holy Grail', suffered the heartbreak of seeing Leicester City's Mike Stringfellow end my Wembley dream in 1963.

But May 1965 was to be the moment. Travelled down to stay with my dad's uncle in Watford on the Friday, most of it via pre-motorway 'A' roads. Couldn't sleep the night before the game – with my thoughts for my younger brother, Andy, who couldn't make it. I did get him a scarf and bobble hat from Jack Sharp's to wear in front of the telly. He still has that scarf to this day.

Got the train down from Watford Junction on matchday in the pouring rain but there was no way that a bit of damp weather was going to spoil my day.

I remember being completely blown away by the size of the stadium as we approached it. I wasn't sitting with my dad that afternoon as we got different tickets because of different 'end' numbers on his and my grandad's season tickets. My seat was behind the goal. When I say seat, it was a number stamped on a long wooden bench, but who cares, I was in!

The game ebbed and flowed but Ee-Aye-Addio We Won the Cup! I was made up for my dad, who had been at the 1950 FA Cup Final and now he would stop going on about them dropping Paisley for that final.

Over the past few decades, I've had the privilege to see the Reds win the FA Cup another seven times but, as the saying goes, you never forget the first time!

John Keith – Journalist, Author and Broadcaster: 1965

When Liverpool met Leeds United in the FA Cup Final on Saturday, 1 May 1965, it was the first Wembley match I reported on as a journalist, then several months away from my 20th birthday.

Growing up on Merseyside as a Wolves fan, bewitched by their deeds in the 1950s and their trailblazing floodlit friendlies against top European opposition, I was witness to the taunts Liverpool fans were subjected to by their Everton rivals – often in the same families – reminding them, 'the other lot', that Everton had lifted the FA Cup twice, in 1906 and 1933.

So, Liverpool's progress to the 1965 final brought with it massive emotional baggage for Anfield fans and also for manager Bill Shankly who termed it a 'disgrace' that the club had never won the FA Cup.

So, for them, and for me, that 1965 final was something special. I was then on the *Bootle Times*, and to go to Wembley and report on the game was a huge moment in my media career, which, at the time of writing this piece, has somehow extended to 61 years. Yes, the magic of that Wembley day, Liverpool vs Leeds United, red vs white, Shankly vs Revie, still lives with me today ... history had been written.

Shankly declared, 'When the final whistle went, I took off my coat and went straight to the supporters. Grown men were crying, and it was the greatest feeling any human being could have had to see what we'd done.'

And, as for me, I was delighted that the *Bootle Times* was one of the first UK newspapers to have the facility of full colour. So, when my article on the final appeared it was accompanied by wonderful colour photographs of an achievement many supporters down the decades had longed to see but never did.

In my memory that colour is as vibrant today as it was on that May day in 1965.

Jordan Wright – Liverpool Fan: 2024

My special Wembley moment has got to be Liverpool's Carabao Cup Final win against Chelsea in 2024. It would be Jürgen Klopp's final 'final' for the Reds!

Liverpool had a depleted squad, with an extensive injury list, which featured five academy prospects led by captain Virgil van Dijk, in what could be argued as his greatest-ever display in a Liverpool shirt. We were joined by an academy scout on the train journey to Wembley who was excited and confident in the ability of our young players.

The young Reds were fearless underdogs, sustaining attack after attack from a well-established Chelsea side who hit everything but the back of the net! The game was very tense and eventually decided in extra time by a towering Virgil van Dijk header: 1-0.

The fans were world-class, in full voice and support for the 'Klopp Kids'! A sea of red flags, scarves and smoke – a special day for Liverpool FC and the Liverpool FC Academy in equal measure.

John Thompson – Former Sports Editor of the *Liverpool Daily Post and Echo*: 1989

Saturday, 20 May 1989. And the third Wembley cup final between Liverpool and Everton in five years. In my 20s I'd been to all of the Reds' Wembley finals in a minibus with Kopite pals and my younger brother, Mike. But now it struck me, it was high time to take Dad, now coming up for 65, with us.

John Henry Thompson had never seen Liverpool win the FA Cup. He went to Wembley on a train in the rain in 1950 to see Arsenal win 2-0 against a side containing an injured Billy Liddell. And my nan died less than 24 hours before the 1965 final, meaning he missed the victory over Leeds United. He spent that day instead consoling Mum.

At 6am, I drove Dad down with me in 1989, shortly after the Hillsborough disaster, of course. We'd silently laid scarves together on the Kop weeks earlier. I will always remember the look on Dad's face when we met up with the lads in a hotel in Harrow with time still for breakfast, and with one or two pals (it might have been more) favouring a pint over an orange juice, even at 9am.

Another classic all-Merseyside final ensued, as we know. A 3-2 victory for the Reds saw Ronnie

Whelan hoist the trophy and I was chuffed for Dad more than anything else. He'd finally seen his beloved Liverpool win the FA Cup.

Dad died in June 2014, just before his 90th birthday. But knowing he was there with Mike and me, with us all at Wembley for the famous and poignant Merseyside occasion, still brings a smile to my face. And a tear to my eye.

Andy Proudfoot – Lifelong Liverpool Fan: 1965/79/83

I have picked three matches across three different competitions that were the most special Wembley occasions for me as a Liverpool fan since the early 1960s.

Liverpool 2, Leeds United 1, 1965 FA Cup Final – impossible to overstate the importance of this game in the history of the club. Our first FA Cup win, a huge monkey off our back. An emotional day all around. I watched it on the telly and I still have the scarf my brother, Ross, bought me to wear on the day. And I've worn it ever since!

Liverpool 3, Arsenal 1, 1979 FA Charity Shield – an absolute masterclass performance by the reigning league champions. Three terrific goals. Dalglish in his pomp, rarely bettered.

Liverpool 2, Manchester United 1, 1983 Milk Cup Final – I can clearly remember the sense of ecstatic relief when Alan Kennedy fired in the equaliser. Great game, belting goal from Ronnie Whelan, and Bob Paisley collects our third League Cup win. Fantastic memories.

Dave Ball – Liverpool Fan and Stats Man: 1989

As a member of the Radio Merseyside team, I was tasked with providing players from both sides for interviews before and after the 1989 FA Cup Final. As a serving Liverpool schoolteacher, and research consultant on TV's *Question of Sport* back then, I found it relatively straightforward as I had met many of the players on numerous occasions.

At 2.45pm I was summoned back to the commentary areas but stayed put as the teams emerged from the dressing rooms, and I followed them as they reached the pitch. The crescendo of noise is something I have not witnessed since.

Returning to my seat, I left for the tunnel some three minutes before what I hoped would be the conclusion of the game, with the Reds one goal ahead. As I entered the playing area, a massive roar shook me, and I believed the trophy had been secured, only to see a mass of blue scarves ahead of me as the Toffees had just equalised.

I made the same journey a minute or so before the final whistle was blown after extra time, Rushie's two goals ensuring a fourth success in the competition.

My fondest memory, and indeed the saddest, was when Gary Ablett, the captain of my Liverpool Schoolboys team a few years before, put his arms around me and told me about the journey from Penny Lane (home of the Boys team) to Wembley. Gary sadly died on New Year's Day in 2012 after a battle with non-Hodgkin's lymphoma at the age of 46, but he is a major part of Wembley history as the only player to win the FA Cup with both the Reds and the Blues.

Steve Rotheram – Metro Mayor Liverpool City Region: 1980

My recollections of the 1980 FA Charity Shield match between Liverpool and West Ham United centre around the generosity of a Liverpool player – and my attempts to impress a girl.

I was an apprentice bricklayer back then, receiving a training allowance of £17.50 per week, and so a trip to Wembley was a significant proportion of my disposable income once I had paid my mum her 'keep'.

In 1979 I had started courting a girl and was obviously keen on her. One of my friends who was related to the McDermott family had provisionally reserved seats on a coach to the match in London and was taking his girlfriend. I wanted to follow suit with my girlfriend, but first needed to borrow some money. My financial saviour, as always, was the 'Bank of Mum'. Despite being unlikely to be able to pay her back for many months, Mum lent me £40 to pay for tickets, travel, food and drink.

The match itself is a bit of a blur, although we did win with a first-half goal from short range by Terry McDermott. At the end of the game, we seemed to wait for ages before the coach was ready to leave Wembley and take us on the journey home, when suddenly Terry McDermott jumped on the bus to join us. Terry was a fantastic footballer, and as a Kirkby lad myself I always had a certain affection towards him.

Who wouldn't want to be Terry McDermott? His brother, Peter, then announced to everyone on the coach that Terry would pay for everyone's tickets, as scoring the winning goal he would receive a win and goalscoring bonus. I thought I'd won the pools. I was buzzing as I had bought two tickets, which I would now get my money back from – and this would mean more money to buy a few extra lagers. Happy days, I thought!

Many decades later, I regaled this story to Terry at a Lady Marina Dalglish Charity Ball at Knowsley Hall. By my side was the girl who I took to Wembley on that day, now my wife of 30 years and mother of our three children. Terry was still charming, with a sharp sense of humour. 'Your round then,' he said. 'No problem, what are you drinking?' I enquired. 'A bottle of champagne,' he told me with a wry grin on his face and his arms outstretched. 'Bargain,' I replied as I ordered his chosen tipple. My attempts to impress my teenage girlfriend had been successful, which, in some part, was due to a trip to Wembley and the Charity Shield match 40-odd years earlier. Not a bad deal.

Even with inflation, a bottle of Möet didn't go close to paying him back. But I'll never forget the generosity of a true Liverpool legend and top Scouser.

Ged Rea – Liverpool Fan and Stats Man: 1978

Wembley Stadium. The original Wembley. One of the great cathedrals of world sport and it had to be the ambition of every football fan to see his team play there. And as a 14-year-old in 1978 I was granted my wish.

Tickets were difficult to source and lucky for me one of my close school pals was on Liverpool's books as a schoolboy. But as a rabid Blue, he did not wish to be one of the 100,000 fans inside the ground for the 1978 League Cup Final between Liverpool and Nottingham Forest. My seat was even among the party of club apprentices, high up in the side – the Royal Box side. Thanks, Murph!

This over-excited youngster could not wait for the big day and when it arrived set off on a four-hour motorway drive with friends. Nottingham Forest would pose the sternest of tests. They were newly promoted but top of the league with Liverpool one place below.

The Wednesday before, the Reds had booked a place in the European Cup semi-finals thanks largely to a calamitous performance from Benfica goalkeeper Bento at Anfield. This time, the opposition goalkeeper was to be our nemesis. Chris Wood was 18 years old and was only playing because Peter Shilton was cup-tied. He made a string of fine saves and the only time he was beaten, by a Terry McDermott shot, a linesman's flag saved him.

Liverpool should have won comfortably, but the day failed to produce a goal. The final was going to a replay at Old Trafford the following Wednesday. The feeling coming out of the stadium on 18 March was that it would be the first of many visits for me, and Liverpool FC have not let me down.

Debbie Hewitt – FA Chair and Liverpool Fan: 2022

Being asked to write about my favourite Liverpool game at Wembley was more difficult than I thought it would be. I changed my mind many times. It had to be one I watched with my dad;

after all, he'd introduced me to football all those years ago, although he was a Notts County supporter, not a Liverpool fan.

My choice? The 2022 Carabao Cup Final – Chelsea vs Liverpool – which represents so much about Liverpool FC and my own personal football journey. Despite Jürgen Klopp's record-breaking tenure, including Champions League and Premier League triumphs, Liverpool had not won a domestic final since 2012. Our route to the final wasn't easy. We found ourselves 3-1 down to Leicester City in the fifth round. It was prophetic that the game concluded with a penalty shoot-out, and a spectacular save from Caoimhín Kelleher. We beat my daughter's favourite team, Arsenal, in the semi-final, but her twin brother is a fanatical Liverpool fan like his mum, and we were off to Wembley for our 13th League Cup Final … 13 has always been my lucky number.

27 February 2022 – Chelsea made the stronger start, but it remained 0-0 at half-time. Matip scored a superb header in the 69th minute but it was ruled offside. Extra time saw Chelsea denied two goals, Lukaku and Havertz also both ruled offside.

The inevitable penalty shoot-out followed, with Chelsea having substituted their goalkeeper, Mendy, for Arrizabalaga. Both sides converted their penalties, 10-10, and so the goalkeepers got their chance to score rather than save. Kelleher confidently scored our 11th, and Arrizabalaga stepped up and shot well over the bar.

It took a second or two to register that we had just won a record ninth League Cup, our first of the decade, and Jürgen Klopp's first domestic cup as a Liverpool manager. The game will be forever etched in my memory, although it wasn't just about the silverware. It reflected this great team's ability to handle immense pressure. It was a testament to Klopp's legacy at the club, and for me it was my first Liverpool Wembley final shared with both my dad and my son, the three of us experiencing it together. And it was my first football final as FA Chair. Try as I might, I could neither sit on my hands nor look impassively straight ahead. At least it was not the FA Cup Final! That came a few months later …

Graham Webster – Lifelong Liverpool Fan: 1978

Having attended Anfield Road Junior School, often stopping off at Billy Liddell's sweet shop on Oakfield Road, it will come as no surprise that I am a lifelong Liverpool fan.

I moved to London in 1974 for a job promotion. Opportunities to see Liverpool, other than on *Match of the Day*, became few and far between. Saturdays spent on the Kop or, occasionally, in the Kemlyn Road Stand had become fond memories. But in early May 1978 an old school friend telephoned to say he had two tickets for the European Cup Final, Liverpool vs Club Brugge at Wembley. What a great opportunity – a European Cup Final at home!

This was my first visit to Wembley, and I noticed the ticket had a seat number on it. I must admit I was very surprised that 'seat' number was carved into a wooden bench!

As for the match itself, it wasn't a great game, but Liverpool had the better chances, culminating in a very special winning goal from King Kenny. Liverpool had become the only English team to win two consecutive European Cup finals, following up their historic win in Rome the year before.

After the game, my mate Mike Barnes and I returned to the hotel he was staying in – the Holiday Inn at Swiss Cottage – and properly celebrated the Reds' Wembley victory at the bar.

It turned out the Liverpool team must have been staying there too, because the players all turned up and trooped through the bar to loud applause from us celebrating fans, and they then set off to their own private room, presumably to continue their own celebrations. It capped a very special day.

***

Over the past six months or so, I've lived and breathed Liverpool Football Club's visits to Wembley Stadium – the 'old' and the 'new'. I've researched the matches, reviewed them on screen, and in many cases remembered watching them in person.

Big wins, tough-to-take defeats and a batch of games that needed penalty shoot-outs to resolve them. Each match has its own story, each outcome has been reflected on many times. Wembley matches, even for the biggest names in the sport, remain as 'bookmarks' in many clubs', players', managers' and fans' memories. Some careers are measured by them.

Our trusty statistics gurus, Dave Ball and Ged Rea, reckon there have been 45 official matches played by the Reds dating back to their debut at the stadium back in 1950 until end of the 2024/25 season. I did a personal check on how many of those memorable occasions I've seen across my six decades of being a Liverpool fan. My conservative estimate is around three quarters of those games – and possibly more, but what writing this book has done is to help contextualise each game, refresh my memory of the occasion, and in so doing given me some confidence in choosing ten Liverpool matches under Wembley Stadium's Twin Towers or Arch (author's privilege!) – and briefly say why they make my 'favourites' list.

And, as they say on all those popular TV shows, these matches are not listed in any particular order – other than by the simple dateline of the match itself. So here goes:

1965 Liverpool vs Leeds United – FA Cup Final: A seminal win in the history of Liverpool Football Club. Indeed, possibly *the* seminal victory. We watched it as a family on our black-and-white TV, and the following day, after I had fulfilled my duty of self-consciously carrying a flag around the local roads at our monthly church parade, we all headed off to Liverpool city centre to see Shankly and his team's own open-top bus parade. They had finally won the FA Cup. Unforgettable.

1971 Liverpool vs Arsenal – FA Cup Final: My first Wembley final attended in person. Sixteen years old, a nervous traveller, my priceless match ticket stuck down the front of my trousers for safekeeping – although that manoeuvre didn't involve a safety pin as well (my mum's original idea!). The whole day was a remarkable experience, a little daunting for a teenager at times, but truly memorable even though we lost the match. And I was delighted to see my mum and dad at Lime Street Station waiting to pick me up at the end of a long day.

1974 Liverpool vs Newcastle United – FA Cup Final: A last-minute ticket secured for me by my dad, a Saturday morning lift down to Wembley hurriedly arranged with 'a mate of a mate' – and a wonderful performance by the Reds as we sang 'Super Mac is only good when it's raining!' Liverpool's third goal, a masterpiece of passing and moving. Shankly in his absolute pomp.

1978 Liverpool vs Club Brugge – European Cup Final: It might not have the sheer sense of adventure for me that my trip to Rome the previous year had, but this occasion was literally the evening 'when Anfield met Wembley'! And our super-huge following in the national stadium witnessed a fantastic winning goal from Kenny Dalglish.

1982 Liverpool vs Tottenham Hotspur – League Cup Final: this was the second match in a run of four consecutive League Cup finals for the Reds. Spurs took an early lead and were ahead until 20-year-old Ronnie Whelan grabbed an equaliser for the Reds four minutes from time. Nothing like a late goal! In a final. At Wembley. We went bonkers!

The young Irishman put Liverpool ahead in extra time, scoring past Liverpool legend Ray Clemence, now in the Spurs goal, before another 20-year-old, Ian Rush, rounded things off with a third goal for the Reds. Whelan, who also scored a brilliant winning goal against Manchester United the following year, and Rush would go on to play a remarkable 1,153 games between them for Liverpool.

1986 Everton vs Liverpool – FA Cup Final: Two years after playing each other at Wembley in the League Cup Final, the two great Merseyside clubs met again on the hallowed turf. I had spent 'cup final' week on Merseyside creating a short documentary about the city's love of football, broadcast at the start of BBC's *Cup Final Grandstand*, and after filming the Reds' team coach on their journey from their cup final hotel to the stadium, I was given the all-clear and afternoon off by my bosses, so I could watch the match as 'a fan' –

the best bit. I travelled back to Speke Airport on Sunday afternoon on a plane that carried both sets of players, before riding on the Liverpool open-top bus itself, going around the city in the company of two very special VIPs – the league championship trophy and the FA Cup.

1989 Everton vs Liverpool – FA Cup Final: It is difficult to comprehend the level of emotion that surrounded this match. Following the dreadful disaster at Hillsborough, the city had come together as one to strongly support and offer a deep-felt sympathy for those who had lost family and friends on that fateful day. Now, the two clubs, who have always represented the city so proudly, were to meet at Wembley in that season's FA Cup Final. Perhaps fittingly, given the circumstances, Liverpool won a stunning final, 3-2, but the occasion underlined that 'Merseyside' would be united in fighting all the way for justice for the 97. The most important match of those I attended down the decades.

2012 Cardiff City vs Liverpool – League Cup Final: Four and a half years after the opening of the new Wembley Stadium and 16 years since having last played there, Liverpool were finally making their long overdue first appearance under the now-famous Arch.

Given my personal allegiances to LFC and my professional connections with Wembley Stadium, it was a day I had been waiting for ... and waiting for! Truth be told, Liverpool made very heavy weather of winning the trophy against Cardiff City. The unfancied Welsh side went ahead, Martin Škrtel finally pulled the Reds level and Dirk Kuyt put them ahead. But Cardiff got a late equaliser. Penalties. And despite Steven Gerrard and Charlie Adam failing to score, Liverpool scrambled home to win their eight League Cup.

And it was another trophy won by their then-interim manager, Kenny Dalglish. And, for me, it was finally a box ticked – the Reds had played at the new Wembley.

2022 Manchester City vs Liverpool – FA Cup semi-final: The titanic battles of recent years between these two titans of the Premier League are legendary. The two clubs under the leadership of Jürgen Klopp and Pep Guardiola set new standards – and the rivalry was rich and rare.

And so to the 2022 FA Cup semi-final between the two teams. When the draw for the last four was about to be made, fans of Liverpool, Manchester City and Chelsea were probably hoping to be paired with Crystal Palace, the other team to have progressed to that stage of the competition – although the Reds had FA Cup semi-final history with the Selhurst Park club. The draw did its business, and the two mega-teams, Liverpool and Manchester City, were drawn against each other. I remember going to the game, fearing the worst but hoping for the best. Many Liverpool fans would have shared those feelings.

The last two Wembley meetings against City had ended in penalty shoot-out defeats. But not this time; on a super-sunny April afternoon with shadows cast long and wide across the Wembley pitch, Liverpool left scorch marks on the turf as they went into a sensational 3-0 half-time lead. It felt great. There was really a good stretch of water between the two teams.

Konaté, and Mané, twice, had put the Reds into what would have seemed to have been an unassailable lead, and although City scored early and late in the second half, it was job done. Chelsea next. And we know how that ended!

And finally, 2024 Chelsea vs Liverpool – Carabao Cup Final: Earlier I explained my late 'fitness test' to make it to this match. A little bit of food poisoning was to blame, but was overcome! This match turned out to be Jürgen Klopp's final match at Wembley with the Reds – and fittingly it was a Liverpool victory.

For me, knowing I was about to start writing a book about the Reds' adventures at Anfield South, I was pleased I had a potentially 'big finish' to write about. More importantly, it was the first big Liverpool match I had been to since fully retiring from the various strands of work that had defined my previous near-50 years.

So, I went to Wembley Stadium that dull February afternoon as a fan, a proper fan, with my son, Jack. No need to 'sit on my hands and look impassively ahead', my tickets were at the Liverpool end of the ground, and I felt very much back at home.

I captured that afternoon with a photograph of Jack and myself a few minutes after Liverpool had clinched victory – with the Arch illuminated in red. That picture is framed and on the wall, staring back at me right now.

Journey's end – or back to where I started. Perfect.

Chapter 10

Facts and Figures; The Story So Far

Youngest to Score

- Ian Rush at 20 years, 144 days in the 1982 League Cup Final vs Tottenham.
- Ronnie Whelan was also 20 years old and scored in that final – 20 years, 169 days.

Oldest Scorer

- Virgil van Dijk at 32 years, 232 days in the 2024 League Cup Final vs Chelsea.

Other 30-Year-Old Scorers

- Dirk Kuyt at 31 years, 219 days vs Cardiff City in the League Cup Final in 2012.
- Sadio Mané at 30 years, six days in the 2022 FA Cup semi-final vss Manchester City.

Two Players Played at Wembley Stadium at the Age of 18 Years

- Jayden Danns at 18 years, 40 days in the 2024 League Cup Final.
- Harvey Elliott at 18 years, 329 days in the 2022 League Cup Final.

Oldest to Play at Wembley Stadium

- James Milner at 36 years, 130 days in the 2022 FA Cup Final.
- Kenny Dalglish at 36 years, 32 days in the 1987 League Cup Final vs Arsenal.

Greatest Span Between First and Last Appearance at Wembley

- Ian Rush at the age of 20 years, 144 days in the 1982 League Cup Final against Tottenham, and over 14 years later he featured in the 1996 FA Cup Final against Manchester United aged 34 years, 204 days.

Appearances

- Liverpool played 31 games at the old stadium before demolition, winning 16, drawing six and losing nine.
- On 25 February 2024, the club made its 44th appearance at the stadium and, by overcoming Chelsea in the League Cup Final, registered their 23rd victory. The defeat by Newcastle in the same competition the following year left their record at Wembley played 45, won 23, drew six, lost 16.

Individual Competition Statistics

- FA Cup finals – won six, lost six.
- League Cup finals – won six, drew three, lost three.
- European finals – won one.
- Charity/Community Shield – won seven, drew three, lost five.
- FA Cup semi-finals – won two, lost one.
- Premier League vs Tottenham Hotspur – won one, lost one.

Most Common Opponents

- Everton – six games (won three, drew two, lost one).
- Manchester United – six games (won one, drew two, lost three).
- Arsenal – six games (won two, lost four).
- Chelsea – four games (won three, lost one).

Five Substitutes Have Scored for the Reds

- Ian Rush (two) vs Everton at the 1989 FA Cup Final.
- Dirk Kuyt in the 2012 League Cup Final vs Cardiff City.
- Andy Carroll in the 2012 FA Cup Final vs Chelsea.
- Jöel Matip, 2019, in the Community Shield vs Manchester City.
- Takumi Minamino, 2020, in the Community Shield vs Arsenal.

Most Goals

- Ian Rush – ten.
- John Aldridge, Terry McDermott and Ronnie Whelan – three.

Ten Different Managers Have Taken the Reds to Wembley

- Paisley – 12.
- Dalglish – 11.
- Klopp – 9.
- Shankly – 3.
- Fagan – 3.
- Souness – 2.
- Evans – 2.
- Kay, Rodgers and Slot – one each.

Other Facts

- Liverpool have now won on four of their last five visits to Wembley, and have won there in five competitions – the FA Cup, League Cup, Charity/Community Shield, European Cup and the Premier League, as well as the FA Cup semi-final.
- There have been 33 different scorers, plus the Gordon Strachan own goal in the 1992 Charity Shield game with Leeds United.
- Six substitutes have scored for the Reds – Frederico Chiesa, versus Newcastle United, 2025 League Cup Final, became the fourth substitute to do so in a final.
- Paisley and Fagan's debuts at Wembley were both in Charity Shield matches – Paisley won in the 1974 shoot-out with Leeds United, while Fagan's first game saw the Reds lose to Manchester United.
- Kenny Dalglish and Graeme Souness played for the club at the ground and then managed the Reds there.
- George Kay famously played in the very first FA Cup Final staged at Wembley in 1923 as captain of the beaten West Ham United team, and 27 years later led Liverpool out for their very first final in 1950.
- Bruce Grobbelaar and Steve Gerrard both scored own goals there.
- Eric Cantona in the 1992 Charity Shield scored the only hat-trick in any of Liverpool's games at the national stadium.
- Chelsea are the only side to prevent Liverpool scoring in any of the club's last 14 visits, doing so in the two cup finals in 2022.
- Liverpool lost only one of the six games against Everton – the 1984 Charity Shield, where goalkeeper Bruce Grobbelaar scored an own goal.

- Liverpool won four games after a penalty shoot-out:

  1974 vs Leeds United, Charity Shield.

  2012 vs Cardiff City, League Cup Final.

  2022 vs Chelsea, FA Cup Final and League Cup Final.

- They have lost in a shoot-out on three occasions:

  2016 vs Manchester City, League Cup Final.

  2019 vs Manchester City, Community Shield.

  2020 vs Arsenal, Community Shield.